Myths and Methods

A guide to software productivity

David T. Fisher

PRENTICE HALL

New York   London   Toronto   Sydney   Tokyo   Singapore

The original edition of this work was published in Germany by Vieweg & Sohn, Wiesbaden under the title *Produktivitat durch Information Engineering*, © 1990 Vieweg & Sohn.

This edition 1991 by Prentice Hall International (UK) Ltd
66 Wood Lane End, Hemel Hempstead
Hertfordshire HP2 4RG
A division of
Simon & Schuster International Group

Printed and bound in the United States of America

Library of Congress Cataloging-in-Publication Data

Fisher, David T.
   Myths and methods: a guide to software productivity
   David T. Fisher.
     p.   cm.
   Includes bibliographical references and index.
   ISBN 0-13-467218-6
   1. Software productivity.   I. Title.
   QA76.76.P74F57   1991   91-14396
   005-dc20   CIP

British Library Cataloguing in Publication Data

Fisher, David T.
   Myths and methods: a guide to software
   productivity.
   I. Title
   004.2
   ISBN 0-13-467218-6

---

2 3 4 5 95 94 93 92 91

This book is dedicated to Mrs. Dorothy Sulzbach who taught me the importance of the written word.

Contents

Preface

Several years ago I had occasion to select a book for training new system designers in my organization. Since my company survives by being able to build large commercial software systems faster and cheaper than the competition, it was very important to find a book that describes which techniques are really effective for designing and implementing software. My search ended in disappointment because all the books I found seemed to overlook many of the practical necessitities of software construction. The most widespread problem was a belief in the myth that software productivity is primarily a technical problem. That is an error. Productivity in the development and use of software is essentially a management problem. The gains that can be achieved, for example, by switching to a new programming technology are usually trivial compared to what can be accomplished by reorganizing the way software is developed and implemented. Unsuccessful software projects fail in most cases because the software does not fit adequately to the needs of the people using it. That is generally a result of poor human communication; software designers misunderstand details about the way an organization really works and are unable to process user feedback in an efficient fashion. These kinds of problems can be overcome by appropriate management techniques. That is the subject of this book. The book explores the most important determinants of software productivity and then provides a step-by-step method for the successful execution of software projects.

The method described has evolved from practical experience. My colleagues and I have experimented with a wide variety of techniques and tools, carefully noting and analyzing our successes and failures. We have discovered that many methodologies actually increase the amount of work a designer has to do without enhancing the quality of the final product. On the other hand, we have come across a number of relatively simple techniques which, properly applied, have a very dramatic positive effect on software productivity. These techniques have to do with the implementation of three basic principles:

1. In order to design a good system, it is necessary to understand the organization in which the system will be used.

2. The most effective way to build anything is to assemble standardized components.

3. The first implementation of any system is a prototype which must be iteratively refined with the help of its users.

In order to apply the principle of understanding the organization an enterprise model is necessary to provide the system designer with a succinct overview of the organization. Much time is wasted in system design projects because designers wait for users to formulate solutions to problems. One often hears an exasperated system designer complain, 'if only the users would get around to telling me exactly what they want'. This very common expectation on the part of system designers turns out to be unrealistic in practice. Users are generally unable to formulate optimal solutions to their information processing problems, although they are quite good at providing critical feedback about existing solutions. Something concrete must first be available on which the users can focus.

For this reason a system designer must be able to create a prototype design on the basis of his/her knowledge of the organization and its data structure. This information can be gleaned from a carefully constructed enterprise model. The book begins, therefore, by showing how a model of an organization can be quickly and easily assembled using structured interview techniques and a computerized repository.

Once a model is available that shows the relationships between an organization's activities and its data structure, it is usually a simple matter to design a software system that maintains the data. All data processing systems offer similar kinds of services; data elements are inserted, altered, deleted and viewed. In addition, a relatively small number of specific transformations of the data are available. Such commonalities can be exploited for the standardization of software modules in ways that facilitate their reusability. That simplifies design, construction and use of software systems. For this reason the book discusses techniques for the design and use of reusable software components which can raise programmer productivity by as much as 500 per cent.

No matter how much effort is put into the planning of a system, the initial version will inevitably have to be improved. The realistic designer, therefore, considers every new system to be a prototype which must be iteratively refined. The success of the refinement process is, however, critically dependent on the efficient application of appropriate management techniques. The book, therefore, concludes with a discussion of how to manage the refinement process with the help of a user committee.

Enterprise modelling, reusable software components and iterative refinement of prototypes with the help of user committees are and will remain the keys to high software productivity. As technology advances, the way these techniques are implemented will evolve, but the basic management approach will stay the same because the essential problems of human communication are timeless.

David T. Fisher
March 1991

1 The Problem of Productivity in Information Systems

Software is the most important instrument for improving efficiency that the Industrial Age has produced. If properly used, it can provide remarkable competitive advantages. This potential is rarely fully exploited, however, because most software is developed inefficiently and used inappropriately. This need not be the case. Forty years of experience with information technology have produced a formidable array of techniques for increasing the probability of success of software projects. Despite rapid changes in information technology these methods retain their relevance. This book investigates the important determinants of software productivity and presents a software development method based on the most effective and practical information engineering techniques.

1.1 The Importance of Software Productivity

1.1.1 Information Systems and Economic Efficiency

The most important goal of information technology is the increase of economic efficiency. The principal instruments for achieving this goal are computers and software systems (Fig.1.1). Through the use of these

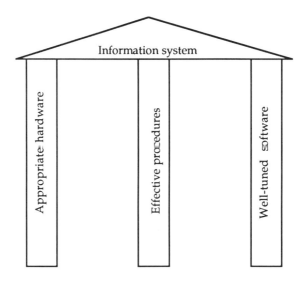

Figure 1.1: The three pillars of a good information system

instruments firms strive to optimize organizational procedures and decision-making. Optimality in this case means adherence to the economic principle: to achieve the maximum benefit with a given level of expenditure or a given level of benefits with the minimum expenditure. In theory data processing techniques are applied in order to bring organizational procedures into line with the economic principle. In practice such attempts fail surprisingly frequently. A recent Diebold study of the use of data processing in about seventy industrial and service companies in Austria, Germany and Switzerland showed that two-thirds of the firms surveyed achieved no measurable increase in productivity through the use of data processing.[1]   This study was primarily concerned with office automation. The main reasons for failure were lack of user satisfaction and inability of the systems to meet organizational needs. Although these results may seem surprising, experienced systems builders know that they are typical and not only in the area of office automation.

There are many reasons for this sorry state of affairs. The most important one, however, has to do with the fact that information systems frequently do not fit well into the organizations they are supposed to support. The results range from disgruntled users to computerized chaos. The organization of a firm and its information system are inextricably intertwined: one must be fine-tuned to the other. It is quite amazing how infrequently this occurs. Often this has to do with a kind of technological fetishism; the computer is seen to have almost magical properties. The mere presence of high tech equipment is believed to guarantee success. Guided by the latest fashions and buzz words many managers approve huge expenditures without any firm idea of what is to be improved and how. Tools are purchased without a precise conception of what they will be used for. It is as though a carpenter first buys a hammer and then looks to see if there are any nails that need to be driven in. Under these circumstances it is no wonder that so many projects achieve so little.

1.1.2 The Financial Impact of Software Productivity

Problems with information systems (IS) usually have more to do with software than with hardware. The hardware components of computer systems are fairly independent of the applications; mistakes can be easily remedied (e.g. buy more disks or memory). In addition the enormous productivity gains in the manufacturing of hardware have resulted in a cost reduction trend which makes hardware an ever-smaller proportion of the total IS budget. Through standardization and automation of hardware manufacturing the price/performance ratio of most computer systems halves about every two years. There are few business areas with such dramatic productivity gains. On the software side, however, things are very different. Software development resembles in many ways hardware manufacturing in the 1950s. Custom-built components are fitted together in labour-intensive ways to produce unreliable products requiring high maintenance costs. Poor software development techniques and the resulting low-quality software are, therefore, the main sources of difficulty. This is particularly unfortunate inasmuch as software is rapidly becoming one on the most significant cost factors for many businesses. In 1985 about

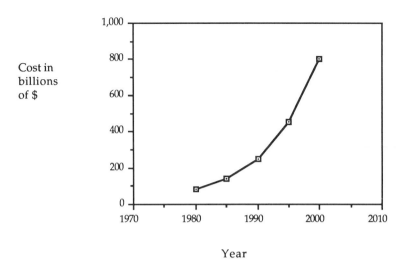

Figure 1.2: Trend curve for software costs

$140 billion were spent on software world-wide.   At the current rate of
growth (about 12 per cent per year) this figure will rise to about $450 billion
by 1995 (Fig.1.2).[2] At these enormous levels of expenditure even tiny
improvements in productivity will have a very significant aggregate
impact. Productivity improvement in the development and use of software
is, therefore, a major business concern.

1.2 The Analysis of the Elements of Software Productivity

1.2.1 The Important Determinants of Efficiency

The major problem in information systems development has to do with
the discrepancies between business realities and software systems. All other
problems such as lack of user satisfaction are derived from this one basic
problem. Such discrepancies are in evidence both with standard packages
and custom-built systems. During implementation software is frequently
found to be inadequate, resulting in an unplanned but unavoidable

increase in cost, because the system must be improved, enhanced or possibly even replaced. It is the loss of software cost control (the implementation of software packages is treated here as a special case of software development) that destroys the gain in efficiency. It is not that the software is useless, but that the benefits are simply not great enough to cover the unanticipated increase in development costs. In order to keep control of software projects it is appropriate, therefore, to scrutinize software development costs with an eye toward reducing them wherever possible.

The Human Factor

The analysis of software costs can be conducted in a number of ways. One very effective method concentrates on those attributes of software projects which affect development costs. These attributes, the so-called cost drivers, have different levels of significance. Fig. 1.3 shows sixteen different factors which have been shown to affect software development costs. Many of these factors (unfortunately not all) can be altered by appropriate management action. These factors are taken from an empirical study of software development projects and software maintenance projects.[3] Each factor is a cost multiplier expressing the relative effect that this factor can have on the total cost of a project. For example developing a software system in a language with which the programmers are not familiar can result, all other things being equal, in a 20 per cent increase in the number of hours needed for the project. The relatively small impact of language knowledge is an important fact which is not intuitively obvious. Judging by the advertisements for programmers it would seem that data processing managers tend to overemphasize specific language experience as well as application experience. A much more important factor is the overall ability (intelligence and motivation) of the applicants. In this case the multiplier is 4.18, i.e. a mediocre team will need over four times as long as a first class team to complete a project. If the choice is between an average programmer with relevant language and applications experience and a really gifted programmer without such experience, it is usually a mistake to choose the more experienced candidate! In general it is always a good idea to pick

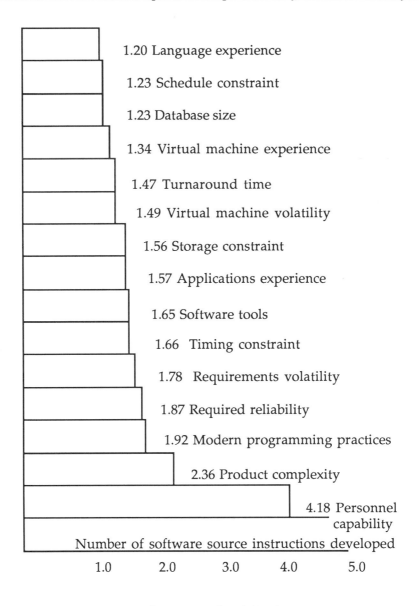

Figure 1.3: Software productivity factors

brilliant employees, because productivity ranges are much greater than salary ranges.

The Impact of the Scope of the System

By far the most important factor affecting software development costs is the number of deliverable source code instructions. The impact of this factor is open-ended; the bigger the system, the more expensive it is going to be. Attempts to reduce the number of source code instructions to be developed constitute, therefore, an important part of any strategy for improving productivity. One of the ways to approach this is to use modern programming languages. For this reason so-called fourth generation languages (4GLs)[4] have evoked widespread interest in the last few years. Practical experience with these languages seems to indicate, however, that 4GLs create almost as many problems as they solve. Table 1.1 compares the touted advantages of 4GLs with the problems that can arise under real-world conditions.[5] Such languages make it possible to program certain types of applications quickly and easily. They usually also make testing much simpler by providing a well-integrated development environment. With more complex applications, however, the programming can turn out to be more difficult than with a traditional language. This is because 4GLs often have very irritating restrictions for such things as module size and size of internal tables. Getting around these restrictions sometimes involves writing more code than would be necessary in Cobol or PL/1!

Another serious disadvantage of 4GLs has to do with the fact that there are no generally accepted standards. That means that the user is totally subject to the whims of the 4GL supplier about what the language is really supposed to be able to accomplish. This is exacerbated by the competitive situation among suppliers which frequently results in the premature distribution of products which have not been adequately tested. One very well known 4GL supplier, for example, continued for more than a year after the initial appearance of his product to issue new versions every few weeks. The supplier was forced to do this because each version had such serious bugs that customers demanded immediate corrections. The problem was that each new version contained new bugs as well as incompatibilities with earlier versions. Software developers who had the misfortune to have to use the product during this period suffered great frustration because, with each new version, the programmers would have

Table 1.1: Comparison of the advantages and disadvantages of 4GLs

Putative advantages	Disadvantages that can arise in practice
Easy to use	Easy to use only if you stick to the things that the language was specifically designed to handle
Can be used by non-technical users to obtain results	Such results are often highly unreliable
Employs a database management system directly	One poorly formulated query can hang up the whole system
Requires significantly fewer instructions than Cobol	Only if you do not run into the 4GL's limitations
Non-procedural code used where possible	This often limits the flexibility of the programmer
Intelligent default assumptions made about what the user wants, where possible	The assumptions are often incorrect
Designed for on-line operation	So are the other languages
Enforces or encourages structured code	Also enforces unrealistic limitations of such things as table size and module size
Subset can be learned by non-technical users in a two-day training course	Such subsets can usually only handle trivial tasks which are not a problem anyway
Designed for easy debugging	Most of the debugging time is spent getting around the bugs of the 4GL
Results obtained in considerably less time than with Cobol or PL/1	Significant productivity gains are frequently not in evidence

to design some fix to get around a particular bug. Then a new version would arrive and the fixes would no longer work! Many of the programs then had to be rewritten at great expense. Under these circumstances it is not surprising that some customers flatly refused to accept new releases of the product, preferring to work with a faulty but understood version of the software. The maturing of a programming language takes years and is usually accompanied by a gradual increase in functionality. Through the feedback of dissatisfied users the supplier realizes what must still be built into the language in order to make it really useful. That means when the 4GL is finally mature, it is as large and comprehensive as a 3GL and no longer simpler and easier to learn.

The advantages of simplicity and easy learnability are also supposed to make it possible for end users to write their own programs. Many over-burdened data processing managers hope that 4GLs, usually in combination with relational databases, will allow them to shift part of the programming burden to users.[6] This turns out in most cases to be very unrealistic unless the user department happens to have qualified programmers among its personnel. Without this kind of expertise, end user programming can turn out to be one of the most dangerous experiments in which a company can get involved. Even simple 4GLs presume logical abilities and understanding of data structures that are rare enough even among programmers. In order to understand the results of queries the user must, for example, have a thorough understanding of Boolean algebra. Otherwise he or she cannot be certain that the subset of the data that was intended with a query is the one that has been extracted. It is very easy to make mistakes like this and not realize it. Such faulty data extracts can lead to serious miscalculations and disastrous decisions. To make matters worse these kinds of errors are usually difficult to reconstruct and verify. The ability to replicate and verify is, however, an essential aspect of a reliable and auditable information system. It is achieved by carefully building controls into the reporting system that prove the completeness and consistency of every extract. It is very unusual to find users with this kind of ability or experience.

Another serious shortcoming of most 4GLs (as well as of many relational database systems) has to do with their inefficient use of hardware resources, a problem which frequently results in unacceptably long processing times. This is a particularly insidious problem which often goes unnoticed during the test phase. That is because the systems usually work well with a few users, but bog down completely when the number of users crosses some threshold. Even with a small number of users, a poorly constructed query can sometimes burden the system such that everything grinds to a halt. In general, 4GLs are useful only if the systems are limited to those types of simple transactions that the 4GL has been designed to handle. The productivity gains have more to do with simplicity, however, than with the 4GL.

The Advantages of Reusability

A much more effective strategy for reducing the number of source code instructions to be developed is the consistent use of reusable software components (and, of course, software packages). The advantages of reusability have been well established in practice. Whereas the average programmer productivity for many years has been less than 4,000 lines of code per year, Toshiba, for example, has been able to achieve rates in excess of 20,000 lines of code per programmer per year through the use of reusable components.[7] Similar results were obtained by the Hartford Group. In an IS department with 1,200 systems developers, Hartford managed to achieve monthly savings of 250 person days through the use of a component library, the maintenance of which requires only 25 person days a month.[8] This library consists of thirty-five documented and tested Cobol modules (fifteen programs and twenty subroutines). Between 30 and 40 per cent of the code of new systems comes from the reusable component library. All programmers are required to use the library as often as possible, to report the percentage of reused code in each new program and to make suggestions for the improvement of the library. In order to stimulate creativity the company gives a prize for the best contribution of the month.

Reusability of software not only increases programmer productivity but also reduces the fault rate of the developed modules (Figs. 1.4 and 1.5).

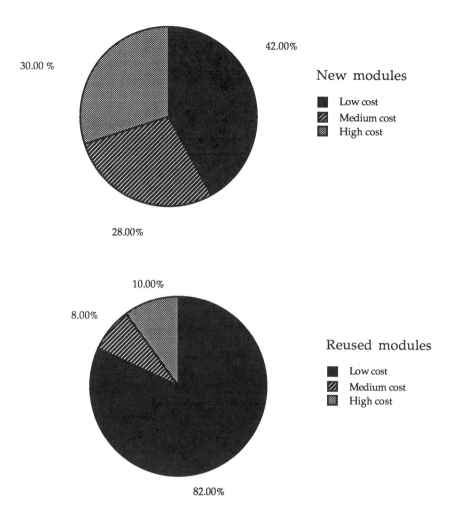

Figure 1.4: Comparison of the development costs
of new and reused modules

This has been very convincingly demonstrated by a study of 887 Fortran modules conducted by the Software Engineering Laboratory.[9] SEL is a continuing research project which is run jointly by NASA, the Computer Sciences Corporation and the University of Maryland. SEL monitors aerospace software projects and maintains a database which contains selected statistics from many projects. The study of Fortran modules showed that 98 per cent of reused modules were error-free compared to

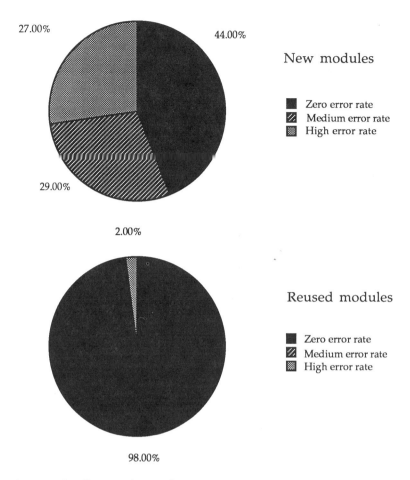

Figure 1.5: Comparison of error rates
of new and reused modules

only 44 per cent of new modules. In addition, this study and other SEL
studies indicate that reusing code requires only about 20 per cent of the cost
of new code.

Another example of the benefits of reusability is provided by
Raytheon's Missile System Division.[10] By supplying programmers with
standardized logic structures this organization has achieved a code reuse
rate of 60 per cent. This has resulted in a 50 per cent overall productivity
gain while at the same time improving reliability and end user relations.

An interesting variation on the theme of reusable code is provided by code generators. A code generator creates programs or parts of programs on the basis of input parameters, saving the programmer the effort of copying components out of a library. A well-designed generator can save much time. With some products, however, working out the parameters requires almost as much effort as writing a program. Real productivity gains with these types of products are unlikely. The most useful generators are those which generate entire programs in the form of easily understandable (and, if necessary, changeable) source code.

Object-oriented Software Development
One of the most promising approaches to the problems of reusability and extendability is the concept of object-oriented software development. Whereas most software development methods rely on the basic paradigm of top-down functional decomposition, object-oriented techniques focus on the data object being manipulated, hence the term object-oriented. The reason for this choice of emphasis is the fact that the data model of a system is much more stable with regard to change than the functions that the system performs. If the system architecture is based on the characteristics of data rather than functions, it will be more robust and easier to maintain. Object-oriented techniques take, therefore, a bottom-up approach in order to develop modules which can be easily combined into many different functional aggregates. The modules are loosely coupled, communicating with each other through strictly defined messages; the implementation details of each module, including the specifics of data storage, are hidden from all the other modules.

These general characteristics of object-orientation are, of course, not particularly new; such concepts as bottom-up design and information hiding have always been important in software development approaches that involve reusable components. The real innovation lies in the attempt by object-oriented techniques to solve one of the most basic problems of reusability, the adequate specification of truly general-purpose modules. Even when processes are very similar, there is still always an enormous amount of variability in the possible implementations. Capturing the commonality of the processes without getting bogged down in the specifics of a particular implementation becomes a major difficulty. The dilemma here results from the necessity of achieving a complete, precise and unambiguous description of the module, but in such a way that a client module can use it without knowing its implementation details (field types and lengths, access techniques, etc.). This dilemma is solved by the concepts of class and abstract data type. A class is a set of data structures characterized by common properties; an abstract data type specification describes a class in terms of the services which can be performed on the data structures and not in terms of the implementation details of those data structures. A table might be defined, therefore, as a class of data structures in which an element can be stored, accessed or deleted. Neither the characteristics of the element nor the internal organization of the table need necessarily be specified. In this way a module is defined rigorously but on a high enough level of abstraction that it can be used for many different purposes. This kind of module specification is an external view; the internal details remain invisible to the other modules in the system.

The basic building blocks of an object-oriented system can thus be viewed as bundles of data and code. Each such bundle is a class and communicates with other classes in strictly defined ways. These classes have two types of relationship: client and descendant. A class A is said to be a client of class B if it uses class B's services. Class A is a descendant of class B if it extends or specializes the services offered by class B. This second type of relationship is also known as inheritance and is one of the most powerful technical innovations of object-oriented programming languages. Inheritance makes it possible to postpone the detailed specification of an implementation until the very last minute. That means that most parts of any system under development can be constructed without prematurely finalizing those aspects that make the system unique. Since the unique aspects of the system are implemented in a small number of modules, the system can also be modified more easily. In order to reap the full benefits of this approach classes must be defined with emphasis on generality and reusability. It is important to avoid temporal dependencies as much as possible so that available services can be pieced together in any desired order. Systems are then created by combining classes in a largely bottom-up fashion.

Object-oriented software systems are best implemented using such object-oriented programming languages as Eiffel, Smalltalk, Simula 67 or C++. Other languages such as Ada and Modula-2 support the type of modularity called for by the object-oriented approach but lack some of the essential features. The most important distinguishing features of object-oriented languages are their ability to support abstract data types and the mechanism for inheritance.

The main difficulty is moving to object-oriented systems development at this point in time is the fact that the technology is still in a rather experimental state. No one has adequate experience as yet of using such systems in conjunction with large mainframes, huge databases and thousands of users. Initial trials seem to indicate that programmers have significant difficulties relearning their trade from this very different perspective. A major conversion effort would be daunting, to say the least. Nevertheless, many experts are convinced that object-oriented software development is the way of the future and by far the most significant productivity innovation that will be seen in the 1990s.

The Advantages of Simplicity; the Dangers of Goldplating

The enormous impact on software productivity of the factors of size (number of deliverable source code instructions) and complexity (2.36; Fig.1.3) suggests that simplification might be a productive strategy. There are few information systems that would not benefit from being made simpler. That is because users tend to overspecify their needs. This tendency has to do with the fact that systems development presents not only technical but also political and psychological problems. Traditional methods of systems design revolve around written specifications of the desired functions. These specifications are usually in the form of relatively abstract documents which the user is asked to evaluate. This is where the psychological problem begins; most users do not fully understand the specifications, because they are too abstract. The users cannot imagine what it will really be like with the new system and have only the vaguest idea of how things are supposed to work. As a result of these feelings of uncertainty, they formulate many requirements which the systems designer then incorporates uncritically into the new system, because he, in turn, does not know enough about the users' environment. Many of these requirements turn out later to be superfluous and only inflate the development costs of the system unnecessarily. The political factor comes into play when users perceive involvement in the design as a measure of their own importance in the organization. In this case users compete with each other to come up with new things that could be incorporated into the design. Again the result is a wasteful expansion of the scope of the system. A related problem has to do with the fact that information systems usually require integration in various forms. The integration of office procedures is always accompanied by a loss of individuality. Employees who formerly worked quite independently of each other must now coordinate their work with others. Each person wants his or her way of doing things to become the standard. This can result in endless discussions which also drive up the costs of systems development. In these ways psychological as well as political factors can lead to overspecification of users' needs. This type of overspecification is called goldplating and is one of the greatest hindrances to productivity in software development.

The Indispensability of End User Involvement
The problems with overspecification of needs and endless design discussions cause many system developers to keep end user involvement to a minimum. That is a mistake. Systems designers usually lack the detailed knowledge necessary for understanding the subtle aspects of the users' environment enough to design the optimal system. In addition user satisfaction, one of the most important factors in the success of a system, is highly dependent on user involvement in the design. An empirical study of 200 users in the manufacturing industry has shown, for example, that there is a high positive correlation between participation of the users in the design process and user satisfaction.[11] This study also showed that user participation in the design process leads to greater use of the system once it is running. That is also important since many systems fail because users

simply ignore them. A system can accomplish nothing, of course, if it is not used. For these reasons there can be no doubt that user participation in the design process is of primary importance. The only question is how to organize and control it properly.

One interesting approach to end user participation in the design process is presented in a study concerning the use of IBM's joint application design method (JAD). The study documents productivity improvements of 50 per cent and more that were achieved by a large US insurance company through the use of a participative design model.[12] The CNA corporation is one of the pioneer users of group design techniques. In 1983 CNA conducted a controlled experiment comparing two software development projects, one using JAD techniques and the other more traditional methods. Productivity was measured on the basis of function points.[13] In the project phases of requirements' analysis and systems design the team using JAD methods required about 2.5 person hours per function point whereas the non-JAD team needed 5.2 person hours per function point.

The Problems with CASE

In recent years a new species of software product has appeared which strives among other things to provide a better basis for end user participation in systems design. These products fall under the heading of CASE (computer aided systems engineering) and offer computerized support of various aspects of the systems development life cycle. This support generally comes in the form of graphic representations of systems specifications. The packages make it easy to create, store and change various kinds of diagrams. These diagrams are supposed to help bridge the communications gap between designer and user. Some of the more sophisticated products can even check for consistency among different graphic representations of a system and generate code on the basis of logic diagrams. The theoretical promise of these systems has, however, yet to be fulfilled in practice. The basic assumption that graphics will eliminate communication problems turns out to be simply incorrect. CASE diagrams are also abstract representations that most users find as difficult to understand as verbal specifications. The typical user has as many problems with an entity relationship diagram as with the corresponding, old-fashioned, written specification.[14] CASE diagrams may help systems designers to communicate better with each other, but not with the average user. In fact the ability to generate diagrams automatically can have the effect that the user gets deluged with piles of specifications and becomes even less able to achieve a proper overview of the system and to participate fruitfully in its improvement.

The hopes associated with CASE are derived largely from the successes achieved by computer aided design (CAD) in other industrial contexts. There are, however, significant differences between the types of problems addressed in each instance. These differences make similar successes for CASE much less likely. Whereas in CAD a three-dimensional object is depicted in two-dimensional space, in CASE an n-dimensional object (software) must be represented in two dimensions. That means that an accurate diagram can become very complex. If, however, making the diagram takes more time than writing the program, productivity gains will hardly be forthcoming. Diagrams in the software context are helpful to the extent that they simplify reality and provide a succinct overview of the problem. CASE unfortunately tends to encourage designers to go well beyond what is really useful.

The problem of goldplating is not addressed by CASE at all. Although some CASE products support enterprise modelling in various forms, these models tend to provide little assistance in setting financial priorities. Typical CASE diagrams depict organizational structure, functional decomposition, data flows, program logic and entity relationships. These documents can be useful for designing a software concept but say little about the economic utility of the system. It is not usually possible, for example, to deduce from CASE diagrams which subsystems provide the greatest potential benefits or which aspects of an organization deserve the greatest attention.

In order to support decision-making concerning IS project priorities, an enterprise model must store quantitative information about jobs, information flows, procedures and costs. Most CASE products neglect these factors. A typical entity relationship diagram shows, for example, the interactions among the various things about which data are stored. It gives a succinct, if somewhat superficial, overview of information relationships. It does not say anything, however, about potential benefits. Fig. 1.6 shows the entity relationship diagram of a trading company. The relationships between customers and orders, orders and the line items of orders, products and orders, etc., are neatly depicted. That can be quite edifying for someone unfamiliar with the organization but does not provide the slightest clue as to what the potential benefits of the use of software systems might be. In order to work that out much more detailed information about work patterns and costs is required. That does not mean that the CASE diagrams are completely useless; diagrams are a useful supplement to any study. They just do not provide anywhere near enough information for a systems designer. Jerrold Grochow, Vice President of American Management Systems, a CASE supplier, aptly characterized the current generation of CASE products when he admitted that the best CASE products today achieve only the level of a junior systems analyst.[15]

Another difficulty with CASE is a lack of standards for passing data from one CASE product to another. Such interfacing is necessary, however, because hardly any CASE product adequately covers all aspects of the development life cycle. To achieve complete coverage it is usually necessary to use several CASE products. The benefits, however, are then severely attenuated, because the various products generally do not work well together. It often happens, in fact, that IS departments acquire such an array of CASE products, development tools, 4GLs, etc., that nobody really has an overview anymore. Training a new programmer becomes a matter of years. The development methodology is less integrated than ever. Any possible productivity gains are more than compensated for by an excessively complex systems development environment. Many IS managers slide into this situation because of pressure to compensate for the low productivity of their personnel. In so doing they lose sight of the fact that there is simply no substitute for good management. It does not help to keep throwing products at this kind of problem. Only a well thought out management concept is capable of achieving superior results with average personnel. This cannot be bought in the form of a package; it has to be

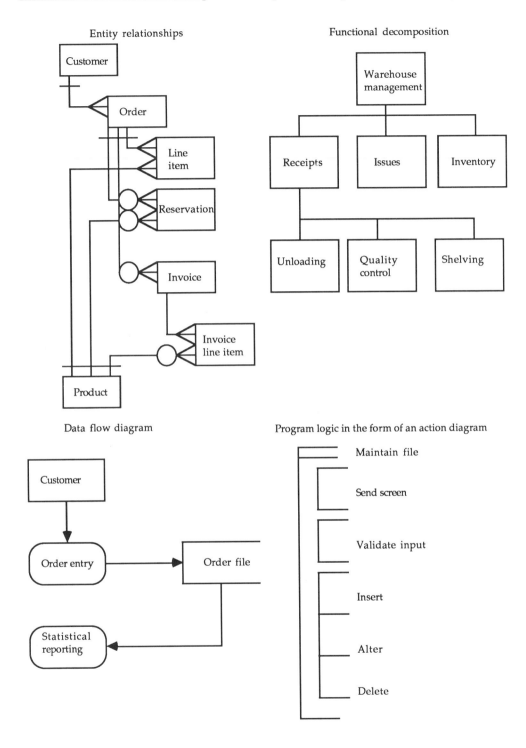

Figure 1.6: Typical CASE diagrams

worked out in detail by the manager. The central principle of good organization is economy. Economy is achieved by first laying out a specific development methodology and then looking for just those tools which are necessary to accomplish the specific needs that arise. In this process a policy of austerity is appropriate, because an excessively complex development environment is highly counterproductive.

The Advantages of Prototyping

One popular approach for avoiding unnecessary system complexity is the use of a prototyping systems development methodology. There are many, in fact, who contend that the initial result of any development project can never be more than a prototype, so that one might as well institutionalize the process and reap the benefits of its being conducted in a controlled fashion. The father of the IBM System 360, Frederick Brooks, is often quoted in this regard:[16]

> In most projects, the first system built is barely usable. It may be too slow, too big, awkward to use, or all three. There is no alternative but to start again, smarting but smarter, and build a redesigned version in which these problems are solved. The discard and redesign may be done in one lump, or it may be done piece-by-piece. But all large-system experience shows that it will be done. Where a new system concept or new technology is used, one has to build a system to throw away, for even the best planning is not so omniscient as to get it right the first time....Hence plan to throw one away; you will anyhow.

This wise piece of advice is corroborated by the fact that the so-called evolutionary or maintenance costs of a system usually make up about 70 per cent of its total life cycle costs.[17] That means that more than two-thirds of the costs of a software system have to do with reworking the original concept. There could hardly be better proof that every new system is really only a prototype.

Prototyping is the best way to solve the problems associated with abstract systems specifications. The users see specific screens and lists and can experiment with programs that really work. They understand immediately what these things have to do with their own work and can make useful and practical suggestions. Working with a prototype is the most effective way to train users and to get them productively involved in the process of stepwise refinement.

There are two variations of the prototyping model, the throw-away model and the evolutionary model. The throw-away model begins with that part of the system about which there is the greatest degree of uncertainty. Experimentation continues until the problem is adequately understood. Then the prototype is discarded and the system is developed more or less in the traditional fashion. The advantage of the throw-away model is the quality improvement that results from having solved the most complex problems at an early stage in the development. Development time and cost are not significantly different from non-prototyping methods. The evolutionary model, on the other hand, begins with the part of the system that is best understood. More and more functionality is then added to this core system until the production system has completely evolved. The evolutionary model has a number of important advantages. A functioning system is available at a much earlier stage in the development process which in turn permits more extensive and productive end user involvement. In addition, it becomes possible for cost/benefit considerations to drive the process of stepwise refinement. For these reasons this book prefers the evolutionary prototyping approach.

Prototyping alone, of course, does not guarantee that a project will be successful. Without careful planning and organization, prototyping can result in premature programming and/or an excessive number of refinement iterations. Premature programming happens when the study of the current system is performed too superficially in the belief that any shortcomings will be discovered and corrected during the refinement phase. That is to be avoided by carefully gathering and analyzing all strategic and operational data that could have a bearing on the planned system. The best way to accomplish this is to use structured interview

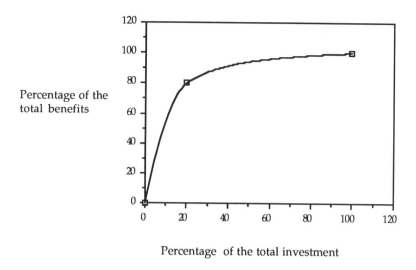

Figure 1.7: The Pareto distribution

techniques to gather specific types of management and clerical information and to store this information in a way which enables extensive quantitative analysis.

   In addition to a thorough analysis of the current system it is also necessary to limit the number of refinement iterations. In particular, it is important to ensure that every improvement of the prototype corresponds to a measurable increase in the benefits. The cost/benefit curve of IS projects generally takes the form of a Pareto distribution, i.e. the first 20 per cent of the investment usually results in about 80 per cent of the achievable benefits (Fig.1.7). It is normally not cost effective to attempt to achieve the remaining 20 per cent of the benefits. It is often difficult, however, to make this fact clear to users. Users tend to think if a function is going to be computerized, then all details of that function must be part of the new system. This, however, cannot be justified economically. Only those aspects of a function for which the marginal benefits of computerization equal or surpass the marginal development costs should be computerized.[18]

Modern Programming Practices

The fourth most important determinant (1.92; Fig.1.3) of software development costs concerns the use of modern programming practices. The major emphasis here is on structured programming which, fortunately, has become widespread throughout the industry. Structured programming is even more effective, however, if it is combined with a rigorous policy of standardization. Naming conventions and the use of function keys as well as all other details of the user interface should be standardized across all software systems of an organization. This policy can be effectively implemented through the use of a centralized library of reusable components. The adherence to standards must, however, be carefully monitored; their announcement alone does not suffice. Programmers are individualists who enjoy tinkering with new and unique programming techniques. Such tinkering can result in creative solutions, but that is unfortunately the exception rather than the rule.

Most individual solutions are not better, just different. To the extent that they unnecessarily complicate the software landscape of an organization, they are highly undesirable. Software development productivity depends to a great degree on uniformity. The rule must be that every programmer either uses existing standards or proves that his or her approach is significantly superior. If it is, then it becomes the new standard. The possibility of defining a new standard normally suffices to avoid excessive demotivation of creative programmers.

Another often neglected aspect of modern programming practices concerns table processing. A good information system is table-driven, i.e. all data that affect the way programs work are stored in tables. Tables are used in practically every information system but often in an inconsistent fashion. The most common use of tables is to store validation information such as lists of valid salary categories, valid project codes, etc. That is important but not sufficient. All data affecting the processing logic should also be in tables. For example, not only should the valid salary codes be stored in tables but also the corresponding algorithms for calculating the salaries. The reason for this is simple. It should not be necessary to change programs just because data have changed. If programs contain sentences such as IF CUSTOMER-NO = '4711' PERFORM PARAGRAPH-A OTHERWISE PERFORM PARAGRAPH-B, excessive maintenance costs are inevitable. If the processing rules for customer numbers change, hundreds of programs might have to be analyzed just to estimate the impact of the change. Considering that maintenance costs typically account for 70 per cent of total systems' costs, it becomes clear that the organization of table processing can be of immense financial significance. In most data processing departments programmers spend about half of their time making program changes that could have been avoided by a proper approach to tables.

Tables can and should be centralized (Fig.1.8). All the tables used by an organization should be stored in one physical data set which is maintained by a single program. Even the layouts of tables can be defined by entries in special tables so that new tables can be created without programming. Centralized table processing offers many advantages, particularly in the realm of data administration. It is much easier to get an overview of the data model of the enterprise and to understand the impact of changes. Naming conventions and consistent use of data elements become significantly more manageable. Programs can be made simpler and easier to maintain. In many organizations, table design is left to the individual programmer. It is a mistake, however, to leave one of the most important information management policy instruments to pure chance. Instead, the organization of table processing should be considered to be an important managerial task.

Another important aspect of modern programming practices has to do with the design of program modules. The study by the Software Engineering Laboratory cited earlier also analyzed some attributes of program modules with regard to cost and error rates.[19] It turns out that some commonly recommended practices are desirable, while others are not. It is often recommended, for example, that program modules be constructed so that they remain within certain size limits. The study showed, however, that arbitrary size limitations can actually increase the costs of a software system. A total of 453 modules were divided into three size categories and three cost categories which were then compared.

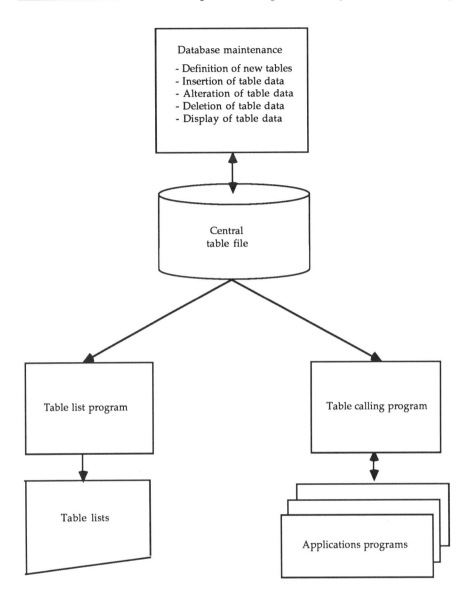

Figure 1.8: Central table processing

It was found that 46 per cent of the large modules but only 22 per cent of the small modules were in the lowest cost category (Fig.1.9). No significant relationship was found between module size and error rate.

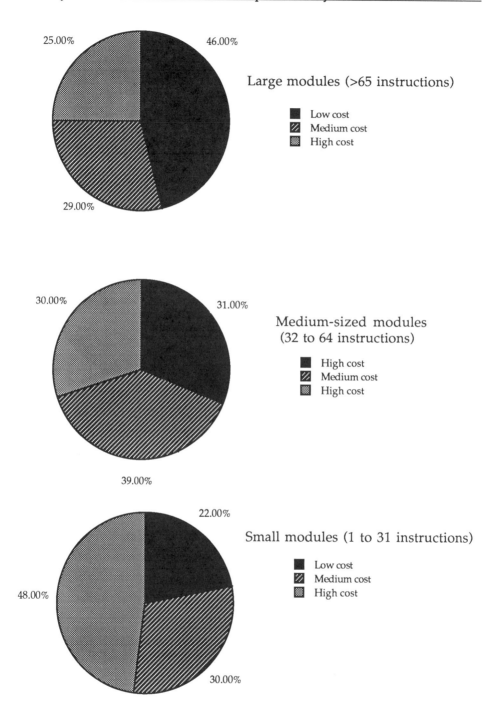

Figure 1.9: Comparison of module size and development costs

Other commonly recommended rules concerning the calling hierarchy and the strength of modules were confirmed by the SEL data.[20] An old module design principle says that no module should call more than seven other modules. The SEL data show that both module cost and error rate tend to increase with the number of called modules (Fig.1.10). Of the modules studied, only 12 per cent of the modules that called more than seven modules were error-free, compared with 42 per cent of the modules that called only one module. The error rate also depends significantly on the strength of the module. A module is considered to be strong if it handles only one precisely defined function. Modules with two functions are of medium strength. Modules with three or more functions are said to be weak. Of the modules analyzed, 50 per cent of the strong modules but only 18 per cent of the weak modules were error-free. No significant relationship was found between module strength and development costs.

Software Tools

The last determinant of software productivity to be covered here concerns the choice of software tools (1.65; Fig.1.3). Hanson and Rosinski have conducted a quantitative analysis of programmer preferences with regard to twenty different software tools.[21] These twenty tools were selected from a group of 400 and represent the typical kinds of instruments that are applied in complex software development environments. The authors of the study asked twenty-five Cobol programmers to compare the tools two at a time and to pick the more useful item in each pair with regard to productivity. The pairwise preferences were then ordered using psychometric scaling methods to come up with the ranking presented in Table 1.2 .

The ranking list shows that the programmers considered an interactive debugger and a screen editor to be the most useful tools. This is not surprising since the primary activities of programmers are coding and testing. Improving productivity requires that precisely these activities be made easier. That is a good illustration of the fact that the selection of relevant tools depends on detailed knowledge of what programmers

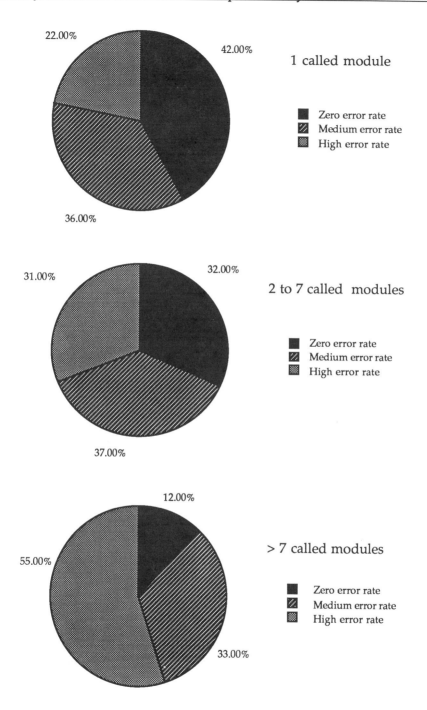

Figure 1.10: Comparison of error rate and descendant count

Table 1.2: Ranking list of software tools

Tool	Relative choice
Interactive debugger	1.00
Screen editor	0.98
Subnetwork checker	0.97
Process meter	0.97
Print file	0.96
Stream editor	0.91
Data dictionary	0.90
Configuration manager	0.90
Source code control	0.90
Test coverage analyzer	0.89
Auto test generator	0.88
Process monitor	0.88
Private library	0.88
Storage monitor	0.86
File comparator	0.84
Big file splitter	0.84
Program cross reference	0.81
Display	0.79
Big file scanner	0.79
Source beautifier	0.78

actually do. Simple as this principle sounds, it is so often neglected in practice. As a rule of thumb an IS installation should first exhaust the possibilities provided by the operating system that came with the hardware. When experience shows that a particular component is inadequate to the tasks at hand, the search can begin for specific solutions to specific problems. This should be done on a need-driven basis with the help of the people who have to work with the tools.

Another important function of software tools has to do with the maintenance of test environments. This activity can have a crucial influence on productivity because programmers spend so much of their time building and rebuilding test environments. It is often necessary to input hundreds or even thousands of records before a test can be conducted. During the course of testing the data are often destroyed and have to be recreated. Under these circumstances programmers often get in each other's way if they are using the same data structures, owing to the difficulty of coordinating record layout changes. Good management often does more to solve these kinds of problems, however, than expensive software tools. With a moderate amount of planning and a few home-spun utilities it is possible to attain a high level of testing efficiency. It is important, however, that the organization of testing is treated as a management function and not just left to the individual programmers. The test environment must be organized such that every programmer can conduct a controlled experiment whenever necessary and then easily restore the pre-test state of the environment. A well-organized test environment; saves an enormous amount of time, not only during program testing but also during systems testing, systems reviews and quality control activities. The organization of testing is one of the primary sources of software productivity improvement.

1.2.2 A Summary of the Most Effective Strategies

The empirical evidence shows that there are many possibilities for improving software productivity. Most of them, however, have more to do with proper management and the consistent application of classic business principles than with high technology. The most important, **proven** techniques for increasing software productivity are summarized in Table 1.3. In the next section a software development methodology is presented which is based on these techniques.

1.3 The Three Phase Method for Efficient Software Development

The three phase software development method is a collection of tools and techniques which enable an organization to attain reliable software solutions in a very cost effective fashion (Fig.1.11). The three phase method is as effective for the implementation of software packages as it is for in-

Table 1.3: The most effective productivity strategies

Considerations	Measures
Personnel policy	• Recruitment policy emphasizing intelligence and motivation • Salary policy emphasizing merit and productivity
Suitability of systems' functions to business needs	• Thorough study of current system using structured interview techniques • Interview database as quantitative enterprise model • Prototyping • Group design methods
Simplification, avoidance of goldplating	• Appreciation of the importance of the Pareto distribution • Marginal analysis of costs and benefits • Need-driven procurement of software and software tools
Modern programming practices	• Structured programming • Consistent use of reusable components • Standardization of all aspects of programs and user surface • Centralized table processing • Strong modules • Limited calling hierarchy • Careful planning of testing and test environment

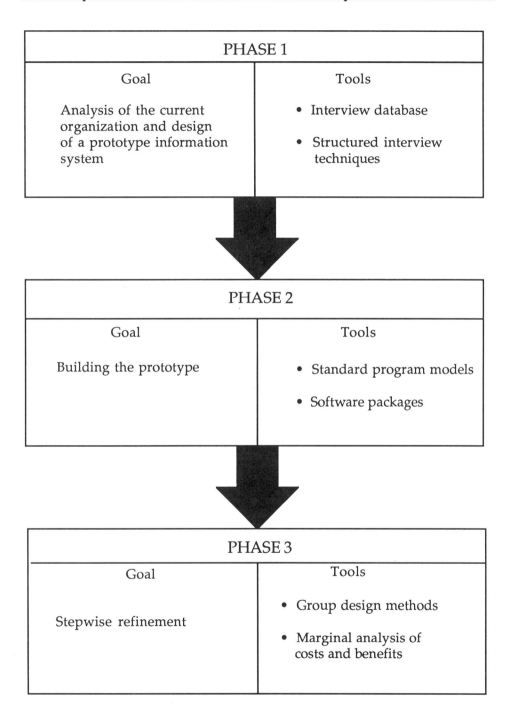

Figure 1.11: The three phase software development method

house software development and can be used in conjunction with any type of computer or language. The three phases are as follows:

Phase 1   analysis of the current system and design of a prototype along with the corresponding data model.

Phase 2   in the case of in-house software development: construction of the prototype. In the case of software packages: selection and installation of the package.

Phase 3   stepwise refinement of the software system with the help of a committee of users.

In each of the three phases the techniques discussed above are used in order to increase productivity and ensure success. In phase 1, for example, structured interview techniques are applied to measure the needs of the organization quickly and efficiently. The results of the interviews are stored in an interview database permitting easy analysis and revision of the data. Quantitative analyses of the contents of the interview database reveal many organizational characteristics which are implicit in the data but which are not intuitively obvious. The interview database is a model of the enterprise which, if properly maintained, can become a permanent information resource, the utility of which goes well beyond the needs of any particular project.

The phase 1 prototype design is done in terms of standardized program models. This approach is based on the proposition that all commercial data processing systems consist of a relatively small number of basic program types. For each of these basic types very efficient models have been developed which incorporate many years of programming experience. By using such tested models it is possible to achieve the kinds of productivity gains associated with standardized assemblies in manufacturing. Through **standardization at the program level** designing and building a reliable prototype can be accomplished in a fraction of the time necessary with more traditional methods.

With regard to software packages, the prototype design serves as a excellent basis for comparison. Although the prototype will not actually be constructed in this case, the prototype design nevertheless represents a detailed representation of organizational needs which makes it much easier to assess the advantages and disadvantages of the software packages considered. The prototype design is also a good basis for discussions and negotiations with the suppliers of the software packages.

In phase 3 the software solution is iteratively refined with the aid of a users' committee. Committees are not usually very good at designing systems but are extremely useful for the critical examination of an existing design. For this reason, a functioning prototype should be available before the committee begins its work. In addition, a reasonably complete interview database should exist to provide a solid empirical foundation for the committee's investigations. The day-to-day efforts of the committee should be facilitated by the use of social science techniques to focus on the important systems questions and to develop specific suggestions for improvement. Since no system is ever perfect, phase 3 can theoretically go on forever. That would be very uneconomical, however, because most of the available benefits are achieved in the early versions of the prototype. It is appropriate, therefore, that management bears the Pareto distribution in mind and limits the refinement iterations accordingly. Since a completely functional prototype is already in place at the beginning of phase 3, the refinement phase can be tailored to whatever budget constraints the firm may see fit to impose.

1.3.1 Phase 1: Measuring the Needs of an Organization

Whether the desired solution involves in-house software development or the use of software packages, all projects begin with the data collection activities of phase 1. These data include operational information about business procedures as well as strategic information about objectives, problems and future developments. The strategic information is collected in a top-down fashion through discussions with managers. The operational information is gathered in bottom-up mode by talking to people at the clerical level. Both types of information are stored in the interview database as illustrated by the schema in Fig. 1.12. Once these data are stored, it becomes possible to use the computer to analyze and display them in a wide variety of ways. These analyses can then be used to facilitate the development of screen and report layouts, program descriptions and a database design for the application system. These documents, taken together, make up the prototype design.

In order to stay within an ambitious budget it is necessary to proceed in a very structured manner. The first step is the development of the interview list which should contain a representative sample of both managerial and clerical personnel who are able to provide the necessary strategic and operational information. Before the interviews start, these people must be informed about the objectives and methodology of phase 1. It is of the utmost importance that the interviewees are properly prepared for their interviews. After that a schedule is drawn up for conducting the interviews. At that point the project manager takes over, conducts the interviews and designs the prototype. The results of phase 1 are illustrated in Table 1.4. These documents succinctly describe the business practices of a company and the information system that fits into its environment. Although it is possible to add much more detail to this set of information, that would only add to the cost of the design without significantly improving it. The twelve phase 1 documents provide an experienced systems designer with all the information necessary to design a first prototype. In addition, these documents describe very precisely what economic benefits can be expected and thus point the new system in the direction of financial success.

1.3.2 Phase 2: Building the Prototype

In phase 2 a prototype system is built and installed. That is the case whether one is developing custom software or implementing software packages. A software package is also only a prototype, even though the supplier might

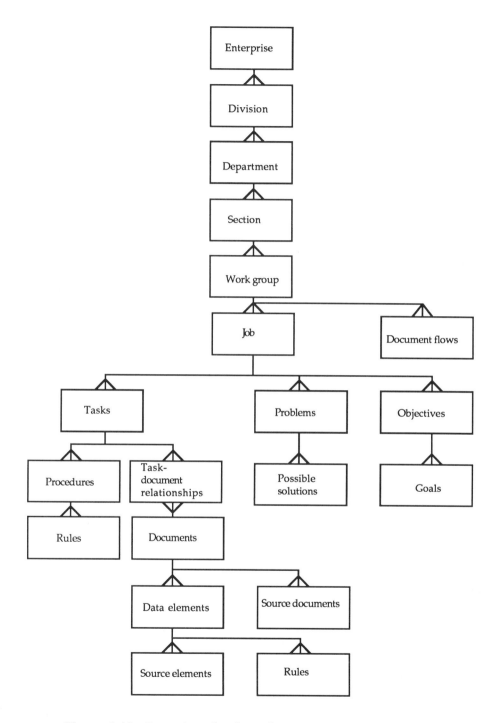

Figure 1.12: Interview database for enterprise model

Table 1.4: Phase 1 documentation

- Lists of goals and objectives
- Lists of problems and possible solutions
- Job-task-document matrices
- Lists of procedure steps per task
- Information flow diagrams
- ABC analysis of information flows
- ABC analysis of potential benefits
- Screen layouts
- Report layouts
- Program descriptions
- Database design in the third normal form
- Job-computer function matrix

be reluctant to admit it. It often turns out, in fact, to be more expensive to adjust a package to the needs of an organization than to develop a custom solution. For this reason the ease with which a package can be changed should be a major consideration in the selection decision.

When developing custom software solutions, it is important to use standardized components. Well-tested models created by experienced software engineers and incorporating modern programming techniques are the best guarantee for quality systems (Table 1.5). If properly structured and documented, such models make it possible for even beginners to construct reliable and sophisticated systems within a reasonable time frame. Adherence to the principle of reusability results in faster development and lower fault rates.

Table 1.5: The twelve model programs

Type	Description	Functional Characteristics
1	Database maintenance program	Each screen has one window. One record can be inserted, altered or deleted.
2	Database maintenance program	Each screen has one window. A scrollable list of records is displayed. Each record can be inserted, altered or deleted.
3	Database maintenance program	Each screen has two windows. Each window has the functions of type 1 or 2.
4	Database maintenance program	Each screen has three windows. Each window has the functions of type 1 or 2.
5	Database maintenance program	Each screen has four windows. Each window has the functions of type 1 or 2.
6	Simple list program	
7	List program with sorting and summing	
8	Transformation program	A file is copied into another file and changed in the process.
9	Transformation program	From one file multiple files are created.
10	Transformation program	From multiple files one file is created.
11	Transformation program	Multiple files are input and output.
12	Menu program	A list of selectable programs is displayed. The user selects one of the displayed programs which is then executed.

1.3.3 Phase 3: Stepwise Refinement

Every software system is initially a prototype which does not handle all the needs of the organization. Despite the claims of CASE package suppliers this will never change. In order to discover all the subtle requirements of a complex organization, it is necessary to have a functioning prototype as a basis for discussion and improvement. An existing system does more to clarify needs than any number of abstract specifications. By working with a prototype, users finally understand what the system is all about and are able to make creative contributions to its improvement.

The prototype should be developed by the project manager on the basis of the interview data. User involvement beyond participation in the interview process is premature at this stage. It is much more effective to wait until the prototype is available to be used as a firm basis for discussion. The three phase method requires, therefore, that a prototype be first developed and then iteratively refined with the help of a users' committee. The refinement process must be constrained by economic considerations in order to avoid goldplating. That means that the marginal costs of every improvement must be justified by a corresponding increase in the marginal benefits. This can be monitored quite effectively in the refinement process, because only incremental changes and not the whole system need be considered.

The political aspects of systems development are an important consideration in any effort to improve productivity. The enhancement of organizational efficiency often involves integration of office procedures, which in turn requires some sacrifice of individuality. This can be an emotionally charged process resulting in endless discussions and considerable conflict. For this problem the three phase method offers fifteen group design techniques (Table 1.6) which help design committee members to achieve a consensus within a defined time frame.[22] These methods promote the creativity of the participants and help them to conduct a rational decision making process.

The three phase software development method is the result of many years of practical experience and incorporates the most effective techniques

Table 1.6: The group design methods

Design methods	Types of project work		
	Investigative	Creative	Decision making
User trips	•		•
User research	•		•
Information search	•		
Objective trees	•	•	•
Counterplanning	•	•	
Interaction matrix	•	•	•
Interaction net	•	•	•
Brainstorming	•	•	
Classification	•	•	
Forced connections	•	•	
New combinations	•	•	•
Enlarging the search space		•	
Functional innovation		•	
Performance specification		•	•
Check lists	•		•

for improving software productivity. The rest of this book presents a step-by-step guide for using the three phase method to develop efficient information systems and to fit them optimally into their organizational environment.

1.4 Review Questions and Exercises

1. Name the three most important cost factors in software development.

2. What measures can be taken to reduce the number of deliverable lines of code? What are the advantages and disadvantages of each?

3. Why do users tend to overstate their requirements?

4. Why should end users be involved in the design process?

5. Discuss the advantages and disadvantages of CASE products.

6. Discuss the advantages and disadvantages of prototyping.

7. Which programming practices have an important effect on software productivity?

1.5 Notes

[1] *Computerwelt* (Austria), No. 17, 9 Sept 1988, pp. 1-2.
[2] B. W. Boehm, 'Improving software productivity', *Computer*, Sept. 1987, p. 43.
[3] B. W. Boehm and P.N. Papaccio, 'Understanding and controlling software costs', *IEEE Transactions on Software Engineering*, Vol. 14, No. 10, Oct. 1988, p. 1,466.
[4] Fourth generation languages were developed to make programming quicker and easier than with traditional languages such as Cobol or PL/1. To achieve this, the languages make frequent use of non-procedural techniques, i.e. the programmer specifies what is to be done but not the detail of how to do it.

[5] The putative advantages of 4GLs were borrowed from the following book: J. Martin, *Information Engineering,* Vol. 1, Carnforth, Lancashire: Savant Research Studies, 1986, p.233.

[6] A relational database system stores records in the form of two-dimensional tables, whereby the relationships among records can be expressed in terms of mathematical functions facilitating access by multiple keys.

[7] E. J. Joyce, 'Reusable software: passage to productivity?', *Datamation*, 15 Sept. 1988, p. 97.

[8] E. J. Joyce, 'Reusable software: passage to productivity?', *Datamation*, 15 Sept. 1988, p. 98.

[9] D. N. Card, V. E. Church and W. W. Agresti, 'An empirical study of software design practices', *IEEE Transactions on Software Engineering*, Vol. 12, No. 2, Feb. 1986, p. 266.

[10] R. G. Lanergan and C. A. Grasso, 'Software engineering with reusable design and code' in *Software Reusability* by Peter Freeman, Washington, D.C.: Computer Society Press of the IEEE, 1987, pp. 151-4.

[11] J. Baroudi, M. Olson and B. Ives, 'An empirical study of the impact of user involvement on system usage and information satisfaction', *Communications of the ACM*, March 1986, Vol. 29, No. 3, pp. 232-8.

[12] A. Gill, 'Setting up your own group design session', *Datamation*, 15 Nov. 1987, p. 90.

[13] The function point method is a technique developed by IBM and is used as a standardized approach for estimating the cost of software development projects. With this method project cost is considered to be a function of the number and complexity of specific application attributes.

[14] Entities are the things in an organization about which data are stored. An entity relationship diagram is a graphical representation of the interactions among these things.

[15] D. Stamps, 'CASE: Cranking out productivity', *Datamation*, 1 Jul. 1987, p. 58.

[16] F. P. Brooks, *The Mythical Man Month,* Reading, MA: Addison-Wesley, 1975, p. 116.

[17] B. W. Boehm, 'Improving software productivity', *Computer*, Sept. 1987, p.48.

[18] Marginal costs are the costs of an additional unit of output, in this case the costs of an additional system feature. The addition to the total benefits that is associated with the additional feature is called the marginal benefit. In every economic context profit is maximized when production is kept at the level where marginal costs equal marginal benefits.

[19] D. N. Card, V. E. Church and W. W. Agresti, 'An empirical study of software design practices', *IEEE Transactions on Software Engineering*, Vol. 12, No. 2, Feb. 1986, p.267.

[20] D. N. Card, V. E. Church and W. W. Agresti, 'An empirical study of software design practices', *IEEE Transactions on Software Engineering*, Vol. 12, No. 2, Feb. 1986, p.267-9.

[21]S. J. Hanson and R. R. Rosinski, 'Programmer perceptions of productivity and programming tools', *Communications of the ACM*, Feb. 1985, Vol. 28, No. 2, p. 183.

[22]N. Cross and R. Roy, *Design Methods Manual*, Milton Keynes: The Open University Press, 1975.

2 Measuring the Needs of an Organization

2.1 The Organization as an Information Processing System

2.1.1 Information Flows

Every organization is an information processing system. The more physical processes are automated, the more significant the informational aspects of the organization become. In order to influence the activities of an organization effectively it is, therefore, necessary to understand the way the organization processes information. In this chapter an instrument called SIABA will be discussed.[1] The use of SIABA enables an enterprise to be described in terms of its most important information processing parameters. SIABA consists of a database, software and a set of procedures which can be used to construct the type of enterprise model illustrated in Fig. 2.1. The SIABA model is used to ascertain quickly the most significant information flows of an organization and to relate them to the overall functioning of the enterprise. In this way it is possible to locate the most promising opportunities for increasing business efficiency and to organize software projects effectively to use those opportunities. The technical details of SIABA's database and software are not important inasmuch as many different platforms can be used to create a repository of this kind. The

Figure 2.1: System for organizational analysis
and requirements planning

significant aspects of SIABA are the data elements it contains and the procedures with which it is developed and used to guide software projects.

2.1.2 Planning and Estimating the Cost of Phase 1

The SIABA model is designed to be used in conjunction with the three phase method described in Chapter 1. The first of these three phases involves two main activities: the analysis of the existing system and the development of one or more proposals for a new system. In both cases a database is filled with specific data items gathered in structured interviews according to precisely defined procedures. These data items are then subjected to various analyses, the results of which indicate very clearly in which ways information systems can be altered in order to improve organizational efficiency.

The costs of the first phase are a linear function of the number of interview partners. During the analysis of the existing system, each users' representative is interviewed twice, once to gather the necessary information and once to review the collection of lists developed from this information. These reports constitute a succinct description of the current situation. If the interview partners are properly prepared for the discussions and the interviews conducted by an experienced systems designer, it should be possible to limit each discussion to not more than half a day. After each interview the systems designer needs a half day to organize the interview results and to store them in the SIABA database. This collection of data represents a snapshot of the organization in electronic form which can be further processed in automated ways. On the basis of the reports extracted from this database, the system designer plans a prototype information system, the main characteristics of which are also recorded in the SIABA database. This activity usually takes about half the time that was necessary for the interviews. That means that the following formula can be used to estimate the time requirements in days for the systems designer in phase 1:

Total time in days for phase 1 = 1.5 (2 x number of interview partners)
                                = 3 x number of interview partners

2.1.3 Modelling

Every model is in a certain sense an abbreviation of reality, i.e. only the significant aspects of a phenomenon are included in the model. This is precisely the advantage of making models. By limiting the analysis to the essentials it becomes possible to obtain an overview of the phenomenon under investigation which leads to a more thorough understanding of its essence. In the case of the SIABA model, the phenomenon under investigation is a human organization. Through the use of SIABA it is possible to present the essential aspects of an organization in such a way that necessary improvements are easily recognized.

2.1.4 Strategic and Operational Data

The construction of a SIABA model involves both strategic and operational kinds of data. The strategic data have to do with the long-term goals of the enterprise and are thus future-oriented. These data describe the manner in which the corporate leadership strives to attain its long-term goals regarding growth, competitive position, market share, profits, etc. The strategies for achieving the long-term goals are implemented through middle- and short-term tactical measures. A medium-sized business, for example, that had up until now always limited itself to domestic markets might adopt the strategic goal of tapping international markets. Various tactical measures might then be derived such as finding appropriate distribution channels, translation of product information into foreign languages as well as increasing production capacity. The success of the tactical measures depends to a great degree on the operational situation of the enterprise. The operational data indicate the current state of the organization and thus represent the basic constraints that will have to be considered when implementing tactical measures. In the example above it could happen that current production capacities are inadequate for achieving the necessary level of output. In order to give a comprehensive picture of the enterprise the SIABA model includes, therefore, deductive elements which relate to strategic data and inductive elements which involve operational data.

2.1.5 Top-down and Bottom-up

Managerial success is achieved when strategies are translated into tactics that result in the desired operational behaviour. That means that the real-life situation must be brought into line with strategic plans. In order to do this, it is first necessary to describe succinctly in a model the current and planned states of the enterprise. Modelling the current state of an enterprise, however, often turns out to be rather difficult because of the vast number of operational details that might be considered. Even in a

relatively small organization there are usually many more organizational
details than one could ever possibly consider in depth. Trying to analyze
them all would mean that the study of the current state of the enterprise
would never end. In addition, the more details that are incorporated in a
model, the more difficult it is to bring the essentials into focus. For these
reasons it is appropriate to start the modelling process with a top-down
approach. Overall organizational objectives are determined and then
broken down into derived goals which are in turn further decomposed
into more and more concrete statements of the plan. In this way a
hierarchy of objectives and goals (sometimes called an objectives' tree)
comes into being which reflects management's vision of the future. The
same technique is also applied to the functional characteristics of the
organization. Every enterprise has certain major functional areas such as
purchasing, production, sales, etc. which act together to achieve the
enterprise's objectives. These major areas are successively broken down
into their respective components, producing a hierarchical structure
known as a functional decomposition. This is similar to the objectives'
hierarchy, but instead of outlining future plans, it reflects the way work is
currently being accomplished in the organization. The comparison of these
two structures quickly yields a rough overview of the relationships
between strategies and procedures in the given organization. Wherever
strategies and current procedures seem to be out of harmony, projects are
initiated to bring procedures back into line with objectives. The
operational data associated with those procedures must be gathered in a
bottom-up and sufficiently detailed fashion such that the success of
concrete improvement measures is assured. A good model must reveal
discrepancies between strategies and procedures in such a way that the
detailed collection of operational data only happens where it is really
necessary.

2.2 Building the Enterprise Model

2.2.1 Structured Interview Techniques

The data for the enterprise model are gathered for the most part in interviews. In order to minimize the cost of the interview process it is necessary to conduct the interviews according to a precisely structured format. The type of data that will be sought in each interview is worked out in detail before the interview takes place. In preparation for the interviews the participants are briefed about the kinds of information they will be expected to provide. Each interview has a specific format which is known in advance to the interviewee, and to which the interviewer closely adheres. The structure of the interviews defines both the questions to be answered and the order in which they will be posed. The structure of the individual interview is different depending on whether strategic or operational data are being gathered. In the case of strategic data the interviews are future-oriented. The interviewer attempts to stimulate the creativity of the interviewee. In the case of operational data the interviews are more oriented to the present. More emphasis is placed on precision and completeness.

2.2.2 Structural and Strategic Information

Since strategic considerations drive the modelling process, it is appropriate to begin the interviewing by seeking this kind of information. A good place to start is the traditional organization chart showing the hierarchical structure of the enterprise. Fig. 2.2 shows a typical organization chart. In this case a five-level hierarchy is depicted. The enterprise is divided into several divisions, each division of which consists of a group of departments which are in turn divided into sections, the sections into work groups. Each work group consists of n employees. The five-level hierarchy is, of course, only one of many possibilities. Different

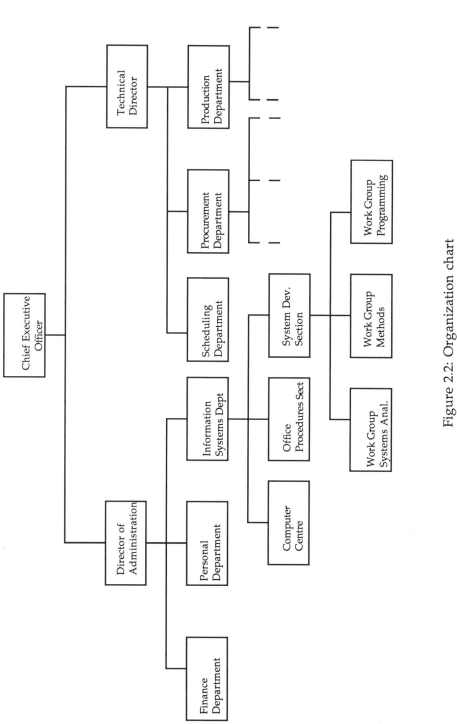

Figure 2.2: Organization chart

organizations have different structures; there are relatively flat hierarchies with few levels and relatively deep hierarchies with many levels. All have in common a basic building block which is a work group consisting of a certain number of employees. It is incumbent upon the system designer to find out how the work groups of the organization under investigation fit together. The systems designer should, therefore, query the initiator of the project about the details of the organization's structure, and sketch an organization chart if one does not already exist. An organization chart is already the beginning of a top-down analysis and provides a good skeleton for the rest of the model. Even if only a part of the organization is to be analyzed, it is still useful to have a complete overview.

The next step in the modelling process is the determination of strategic goals. The organization chart can serve as a guideline for this activity. Every organization has a main purpose for its existence which has been set by owners or legislators. Each unit in the organizational hierarchy has long-term goals that are derived from this main purpose. There usually exists a hierarchy of long-term goals roughly equivalent to the hierarchical structure of the organization. The data contained in the organization chart should be supplemented by data about the long-term goals. To accomplish this, it is usually necessary to interview managers at different levels in the hierarchy.

The emphasis in these interviews is on future needs of the organization. Table 2.1 shows samples of the types of questions that might be asked. Each interviewee should have access to the answers given to these questions by higher levels in the hierarchy. In the course of the discussions it is possible to identify reasonable long-term strategic objectives (Table 2.2). From these, middle- and short-term goals can be derived. The discussion about objectives and goals might reveal problems or weaknesses that will have to be addressed (Table 2.3). In this way the analysis proceeds from strategic to tactical considerations. The information collected in this process helps to identify the work groups that play a critical role in the achievement of strategic objectives or the solution of the most serious problems. It is the operational data of these groups that must be investigated in detail. The initiator of the project selects the work

Table 2.1: Examples of questions for strategic information planning

- What will your market look like in ten years?

- What opportunities will your organization have then?

- What technologies will be relevant then?

- What kinds of problems will present themselves?

- What decisions will have to be made?

- What information resources will be necessary in order
  to solve the problems and make the necessary
  decisions?

groups which appear to require detailed analysis. The hierarchical lists of
goals and objectives and problems and possible solutions aid in making
these decisions. Work groups must be examined in detail if problems are
evident in moving toward the desired goals or if the objectives at
different levels of the hierarchy are not harmoniously integrated. After
establishing which work groups are to be included in the study, a complete
list of interview partners should be developed. This interview list is the
basis for modelling the organizational procedures and recording the
essential operational data.

2.2.3 Procedures and Operational Information

The organizational procedures are mapped by means of an information-
oriented job analysis. Every job in the work group under investigation
should be subjected to this kind of analysis. The main guideline for this
activity is the job-task-document matrix shown in Fig. 2.3. This matrix
illustrates succinctly the relationships among employees, the tasks they
perform and the information required for these tasks. A document in the

Table 2.2: List of objectives and subobjectives

Organization...: XYZ-Software House Inc.

Work Group: Corporate Planning Department

Objectives	Subobjectives
1. Marketing a CASE Software Product	1. Finalize the specifications by 1 Apr. 89
	2. Program the software by 1 Oct. 89
	3. Develop manual by 1 Oct. 89
	4. Develop sales brochure by 1 Aug. 89
2. Triple business volume	1. Place advertisements for additional programmers by 1 Mar. 89
	2. Interview and select programmers by 1 Apr. 89
	3. Direct mail campaign to potential customers by 1 Apr. 89

sense of this matrix is any information medium such as a list, a computer screen or a form. The matrix in the example indicates that Job-1 uses 50 per cent of the average work day to perform task-1 and uses documents A and B in the process. Job-2 spends 80 per cent of the time performing Task-1 with the help of Document D. This matrix can be developed relatively

Table 2.3: List of problems and possible solutions

Organization...: XYZ-Software House Inc.

Work Group: Quality Control

Problems	Possible Solutions
1. Programs have too many errors	1. Additional training for programmers
	2. Increased use of reusable code
	3. Acquisition of testing tools
	4. Reorganization of check-out procedures
2. Poor quality of documentation	1. Hiring of a documentation specialist
	2. Contracting a outside consultant
	3. Training of own personnel

quickly and offers a good overview of the most important informational relationships in the work group.

The next step in the job analysis consists of breaking down each task into its components (Table 2.4). Every task is performed by carrying out some procedure which can be expressed as a finite number of work steps. These work steps should be carefully recorded. One good way to do this is with pseudocode because pseudocode is easily understood by most people

	Job 1			Job 2			Job 3			Job 4		
Tasks	T1	T2	T3	T1	T2	T3	T1	T2	T3	T1	T2	T3
1. Task-1	50			80			20			10		
2. Task-2		25			10			40			10	
3. Task-3			25			10			40			80
Documents												
1. Document-A	•						•	•	•			•
2. Document-B	•										•	
3. Document-C		•	•		•	•				•		
4. Document-D				•								

Figure 2.3: Job-task-document matrix

but can still be formulated very precisely.[2] Some work steps will involve certain rules or algorithms which are necessary for getting the work done. These should also be noted. The rules can be recorded in the form of equations, decision tables or pseudocode.

The job analysis continues with a more detailed examination of the documents. In this step both the physical and logical information flows are of interest. Physical information flows are illustrated in Fig. 2.4 and indicate from where documents originate and how they flow from work group to work group. Logical information flows define the relationships between a given document and its source documents and are shown in Fig. 2.5. Both kinds of information should be surveyed for each document.

The last step in the gathering of operational data is similar to the process of gathering strategic data. Here the problems and possible solutions as well as the goals and objectives of the various jobs are solicited. On the operational level these data might not always exist. People

Table 2.4: List of tasks and work steps

Enterprise.........: XYZ Software House Inc.
Work Group...: Accounting
Job...................: Accounts Receivable Clerk

Task	Work Steps
1. Create invoices	1. Collect and examine time sheets
	2. Check orders
	3. Create and send off invoices
	4. After payment date check payment, remind if necessary
2. Create profit plan	1. Determine indirect costs
	2. Determine project-related costs
	3. Determine open orders
	4. Extrapolate costs and revenues for rest of year

with clerical jobs having few discretional responsibilities do not necessarily have long-term, job-related goals and objectives. They may, however, have problems which are relevant for systems development. Very often people on the clerical level have suggestions for improvements which are creative

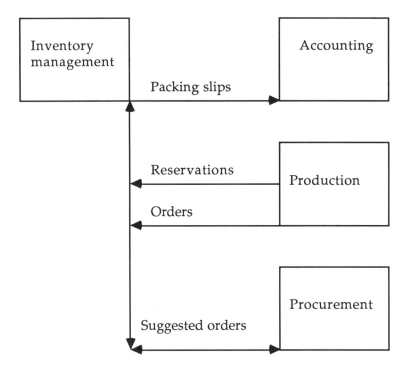

Figure 2.4: Physical information flows

and practical. The information on this level will usually tend to be more concrete and short-term than on the managment level but can be very significant and may uncover problem areas that are completely unknown to management.

2.2.4 The Interview Database

The data described above form the empirical basis for subsequent systems analysis and design. Many significant aspects of the organization are implicit in these data but must first be made explicit. That is accomplished through quantitative analyses. In order to facilitate these analyses it is useful to store the data in a database. The necessary calculations can then be performed by computer programs. The use of a database has other

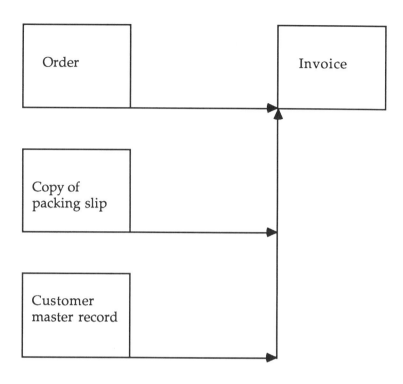

Figure 2.5: Logical information flows

advantages as well. At the conclusion of the analysis of the current system, for example, it is usually necessary to present the results in the form of a report. If the data are stored in a database, the production of the report can be automated. Studies done in the conventional fashion often have the problem that they become obsolete shortly after they are issued because a real-life organization is subject to constant change. If the data are available in the form of a database, they can be updated easily. The report can then be reissued with little effort. In this way the interview database changes the analysis of the current system from a static snapshot to a dynamic, on-going process. The model of the organization remains up-to-date and can be gradually expanded to become more and more comprehensive and informative.

An interview database for the SIABA model is shown in Fig. 2.6. The database consists of a number of simple files which have certain relationships with each other. In the diagram each file is represented by box. The crow's foot symbol means a 1-to-n relationship. An enterprise, for example, is made up of several divisions; each division has several departments, etc. The database schema bears a close relationship to the organization chart from which it was derived. The data for the SIABA model are stored in the files of this database. Each division, for example, corresponds to a single record in the division file, each department to one record in the department file and so on. The database is maintained by a software system consisting of a number of programs. Each file is maintained by a program which can add, change, delete and view records. Other programs analyze the data and create reports. The first six files in Fig. 2.6 (starting at the top of the diagram) store data about the components of the enterprise hierarchy. This example involves an enterprise file, a division file, a department file, a section file, a work group file and a job file. The maintenance program for each file records the data through the use of an on-line screen. The screens for these first six files as well as the data elements involved are illustrated in Fig. 2.7.

The physical information flows are recorded in the document flow file. It is assumed that the most important information flows are those that go from one work group to another. The screen for this process is shown in Fig. 2.8. An information flow between any two work groups can be in several directions: it can run from the first group to the second, from the second group to the first or in both directions. It is, therefore, necessary to input the direction of the information flow.

During the interviews to collect job information each job holder is asked to divide his or her work into a small number of major tasks. In the case of clerical work this usually involves the normal daily work procedures. In the case of management, however, the tasks are typically the decision processes which are necessary for the planning and control of work procedures. Both kinds of information are stored in the task file, the screen layout of which is illustrated in Fig. 2.9. In addition to the task description the average time requirement for the task is recorded as a

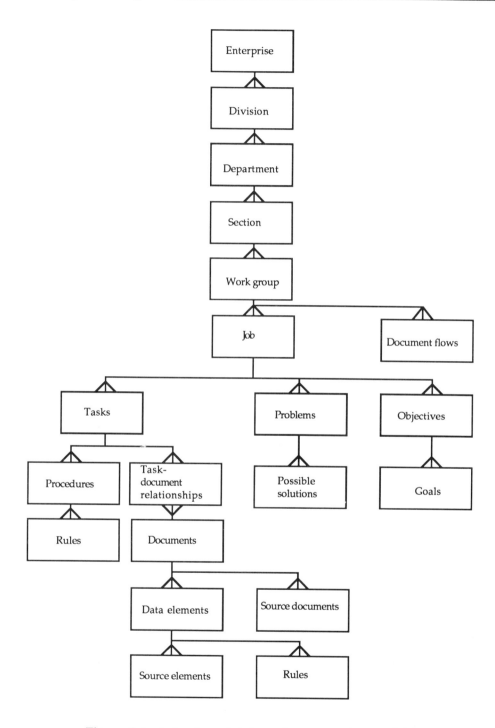

Figure 2.6: Interview database for enterprise model
(reproduced from Figure 1.12)

```
┌─────────────────────────────────┐   ┌─────────────────────────────────┐
│    SIABA - INTERVIEW DATABASE   │   │    SIABA - INTERVIEW DATABASE   │
│        - ENTERPRISE FILE -      │   │        - DIVISION FILE -        │
├─────────────────────────────────┤   ├─────────────────────────────────┤
│                                 │   │                                 │
│  ENTERPRISE CODE:      (    )   │   │  DIVISION CODE:      (      )   │
│                                 │   │                                 │
│  ENTERPRISE NAME:      (    )   │   │  DIVISION NAME:      (      )   │
│                                 │   │                                 │
│  CEO:                  (    )   │   │  DIRECTOR:           (      )   │
│                                 │   │                                 │
│  NUMBER OF EMPLOYEES IN         │   │  NUMBER OF EMPLOYEES IN         │
│  ENTERPRISE:           (    )   │   │  DIVISION:           (      )   │
└─────────────────────────────────┘   └─────────────────────────────────┘
```

```
┌─────────────────────────────────┐   ┌─────────────────────────────────┐
│    SIABA - INTERVIEW DATABASE   │   │    SIABA - INTERVIEW DATABASE   │
│       - DEPARTMENT FILE -       │   │        - SECTION FILE -         │
├─────────────────────────────────┤   ├─────────────────────────────────┤
│                                 │   │                                 │
│  DEPARTMENT CODE:      (    )   │   │  SECTION CODE:       (      )   │
│                                 │   │                                 │
│  DEPARTMENT NAME:      (    )   │   │  SECTION NAME:       (      )   │
│                                 │   │                                 │
│  DEPARTMENT MANAGER: (    )     │   │  SECTION MANAGER:  (       )    │
│                                 │   │                                 │
│  NUMBER OF EMPLOYEES IN         │   │  NUMBER OF EMPLOYEES            │
│  DEPARTMENT:           (    )   │   │  IN SECTION:         (      )   │
└─────────────────────────────────┘   └─────────────────────────────────┘
```

```
┌─────────────────────────────────┐   ┌─────────────────────────────────┐
│    SIABA - INTERVIEW DATABASE   │   │    SIABA - INTERVIEW DATABASE   │
│       - WORK GROUP FILE -       │   │          - JOB FILE -           │
├─────────────────────────────────┤   ├─────────────────────────────────┤
│                                 │   │  JOB CODE:           (      )   │
│  WORK GROUP CODE:    (    )     │   │                                 │
│                                 │   │  JOB NAME:           (      )   │
│  WORK GROUP NAME:    (    )     │   │                                 │
│                                 │   │  EMPLOYEE NAME:      (      )   │
│  WORK GROUP LEADER:  (    )     │   │                                 │
│                                 │   │  YEARLY COSTS:       (      )   │
│  NUMBER OF EMPLOYEES            │   │                                 │
│  IN WORK GROUP:      (    )     │   │  NUMBER OF IDENTICAL           │
│                                 │   │  JOBS IN                        │
│                                 │   │  WORK GROUP:         (      )   │
└─────────────────────────────────┘   └─────────────────────────────────┘
```

Figure 2.7: Screens for recording enterprise structure

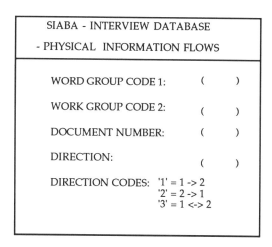

Figure 2.8: Screen for recording the
physical information flows

percentage of the total time expended in the job. The percentages for all the
tasks of a given job must add up to 100 per cent. The time saving deemed
to be possible for each task is also noted as a percentage and expresses the
labour-saving potential of a reorganization of the way that task is accomplished. This is usually estimated by the systems designer on the basis of
the job analysis. This type of saving pertains mostly to clerical tasks. In the
case of management, potential savings are expressed by the next field, the
possible benefits through improvement of planning and control. This data
element records the quantifiable benefits of an improved basis for decision
making. At the time of the analysis of the current system both types of
savings are estimates and are, therefore, input in the fields for estimated
savings. After the implementation of the system the actual values are
input in the fields for actual savings. The last data element in this screen is
the measure of effectiveness for the task. That is a short, verbal description
of how efficiency might be expressed with regard to the task under
consideration. An example might be 'number of vouchers processed per
week'.

Each task can be divided into a number of work steps. These are
stored in the procedure file. Each work step can have one or more rules

```
┌─────────────────────────────────────────────┐
│           SIABA - INTERVIEW DATABASE          │
│                  - TASKS -                    │
├─────────────────────────────────────────────┤
│                                               │
│  WORK GROUP CODE:                  (      )   │
│  WORK GROUP NAME:                  (      )   │
│                                               │
│                                    (      )   │
│  TASK CODE:                        (      )   │
│  TASK DESCRIPTION:                 (      )   │
│  EFFORT:                           (      )   │
│                                    PLAN ACT.  │
│  POTENTIAL CLERICAL BENEFIT:      (  )(  )    │
│                                               │
│  POTENTIAL BENEFITS DUE TO                    │
│  IMPROVEMENT OF PLANNING  PLAN ACT.           │
│  AND CONTROL:                     (  )(  )    │
│                                               │
│  OUTPUT MEASURE:                   (      )   │
│                                               │
└─────────────────────────────────────────────┘
```

Figure 2.9: Screen for recording tasks

which are recorded in the procedure rules file. The screens for entering this information are shown in Fig. 2.10. Practically any number of work steps per task and rules per work step can be entered so that even the most complex tasks and procedures can be rigorously described.

Particular information is required for the performance of each task. This is the most important aspect of SIABA since its main purpose is the support and improvement of information management. This can only be achieved through a detailed understanding of the relationships between tasks and the information needed for the successful completion of those tasks. For this reason it is necessary to store all documents (i.e. information media) in the document file and to relate those documents to the appropriate tasks using the task-document relationship file. The screens shown in Fig. 2.11 are used for this purpose. The document file contains volume information as well as descriptive information so that the size of data flows can be estimated. Many of the data elements shown in the screen for maintaining the document file (from CDC onward) are not relevant for the study of the current system but are used to plan the new system and are, therefore, described in a later chapter. In the screen for maintaining the

SIABA - INTERVIEW DATABASE -WORK STEPS -		
WORK GROUP CODE:	(	)
JOB NUMBER:	(	)
TASK CODE:	(	)
WORK STEP NUMBER:	(	)
WORK STEP DESCRIPTION:	(	)
	(	)
	(	)
	(	)

SIABA - INTERVIEW DATABASE - WORK STEP RULES -		
WORK GROUP CODE:	(	)
JOB NUMBER:	(	)
TASK CODE:	(	)
WORK STEP CODE:	(	)
WORK STEP RULE NUMBER:	(	)
WORK STEP RULE DESCRIPTION: (		)
	(	)
	(	)
	(	)

Figure 2.10: Screens for recording work steps and
work step rules

task-document relationships it is possible to update simultaneously the task file, the document file and the task-document relationship file since these data are normally all entered at the same time.

Each document consists of one or more information fields also known as data elements. If the job analysis indicates that a particular document is essential for the completion of the task, that document should be broken down into its data elements which are then stored in the data element file. It can happen that some data elements are derived from other data elements. An example might be an amount field which is derived through multiplication of a quantity and a price field. In this case the fields 'quantity' and 'price' are source elements for the field 'amount'. Source elements of this type are recorded in the source element file. Since derived data elements are usually the result of arithmetic manipulation of their source elements, the relationships between the two can often be expressed in terms of an equation, e.g. amount = quantity x price. These derivation rules are input into the data element rules file. It is also possible that whole documents are derived from other documents.   An example of this might

SIABA - INTERVIEW DATABASE		
- DOCUMENTS -		
DOCUMENT NUMBER:	(	)
DOCUMENT NAME:	(	)
NUMBER:	(	)
PER		
PERIOD:	(	)
CDC:	(	)
SYSTEM NAME:	(	)
PROGRAM NAME:	(	)
PROGRAM TYPE:	(	)
PROGRAM COSTS:	(	)
ADD. COSTS:	(	)
PROGRAMMER:	(	)
NAME OF TEXT FILE:	(	)
MEDIUM:	(	)
SEQUENCE:	(	)

SIABA - INTERVIEW DATABASE		
- TASK-DOCUMENT RELATIONSHIPS -		
WORK GROUP CODE:	(	)
JOB NUMBER:	(	)
DESCRIPTION:	(	)
TASK CODE;	(	)
TASK DESCRIPTION:	(	)
AVERAGE TIME:	(	)
POTENTIAL REDUCTION:	(	)
MEASURE OF EFFECTIVENESS:	(	)
DOCUMENT NUMBER:	(	)
DOKUMENT NAME:	(	)
NUMBER:	(	)
PER		
PERIOD:	(	)
INPUT/OUTPUT CODE:	(	)

Figure 2.11: Screens for recording documents and
task-document relationships

be an invoice that is produced using the information from an order and a copy of a packing slip. The order and the packing slip are then source documents for the invoice. These are input into the source document file and provide the basis for determining the logical information flows. The data element file, the source element file, the data element rules file and the source document file describe all important characteristics of an organization's information flows and are maintained using the screens shown in Fig. 2.12.

During the study of the current system each person interviewed is asked to discuss problems or perceived organizational weaknesses. These are stored in the problems file. Any suggestions for the solution of the problems or improvement of the organizational weaknesses are recorded in the possible solutions file. The possible solutions can come either from the systems designer or from the person interviewed. They can even be the result of brainstorming exercises with many participants. In any case possible solutions are always connected to specific problems recorded in the problems file. Each interview partner is also asked about his

```
┌─────────────────────────────────┐  ┌─────────────────────────────────┐
│     SIABA - INTERVIEW  DATABASE │  │     SIABA - INTERVIEW  DATABASE │
│         - DATA ELEMENTS -       │  │      - SOURCE DATA ELEMENTS -   │
├─────────────────────────────────┤  ├─────────────────────────────────┤
│                                 │  │                                 │
│  DOCUMENT NUMBER:        (   )  │  │  DOCUMENT NUMBER:         (   ) │
│                                 │  │                                 │
│  DATA ELEMENT NAME:      (   )  │  │  DATA ELEMENT NAME:       (   ) │
│                                 │  │                                 │
│  DATA ELEMENT DESCRIPTION: (  ) │  │  SOURCE DATA ELEMENT NAME: (  ) │
│                                 │  │                                 │
│  KEY FIELD (=X):         (   )  │  │  SOURCE ELEMENT DESC.:    (   ) │
│  GROUP LEVEL:            (   )  │  │                                 │
│  OCCURS:                 (   )  │  │                                 │
│  DATA ELEMENT COBOL PIC: (   )  │  │  SOURCE ELEMENT COBOL PIC: (  ) │
│  VALIDATION RULE:        (   )  │  │                                 │
│                                 │  │                                 │
└─────────────────────────────────┘  └─────────────────────────────────┘

┌─────────────────────────────────┐  ┌─────────────────────────────────┐
│     SIABA - INTERVIEW DATABASE  │  │     SIABA - INTERVIEW DATABASE  │
│       - DATA ELEMENT RULES -    │  │       - SOURCE DOCUMENTS -      │
├─────────────────────────────────┤  ├─────────────────────────────────┤
│                                 │  │                                 │
│  DOCUMENT NUMBER:        (   )  │  │  DOCUMENT NUMBER:        (   )  │
│                                 │  │                                 │
│  DATA ELEMENT NAME:      (   )  │  │  SOURCE DOCUMENT NO:     ( . )  │
│                                 │  │                                 │
│  DATA ELEMENT RULE:      (   )  │  │  SOURCE DOCUMENT DESC:   (   )  │
│                                 │  │                                 │
│                                 │  │                                 │
│                                 │  │                                 │
│                                 │  │                                 │
└─────────────────────────────────┘  └─────────────────────────────────┘
```

Figure 2.12: Screens for recording data elements, source
              elements, data element rules and source documents

or her long-term objectives and the specific, short-term goals or
subobjectives that these imply. This information is stored in the objectives
file and the subobjectives file respectively. The problems file, the possible

solutions file, the objectives file and the subobjectives file are maintained using the screens illustrated in Fig. 2.13.

The files described above are the basis of the SIABA model. Once these data are recorded, the systems designer is in a position to identify the most important information flows and to define a prototype information system. In the process of gathering these data it is neither necessary nor desirable to record all operational details. The files of the interview database should be filled in a particular order so that the selection of the work groups which must be surveyed in detail is facilitated by the data gathered in the initial interviews.

2.2.5 Step-by-step Mapping of the Current System

Determining the Structure and Objectives of the Organization
The first step in the structured analysis of the current system, the determination of the structure and objectives of the organization, is the most important because all subsequent steps depend on this one (Table 2.5). While determining the structure of the organization is usually a trivial task, finding out its objectives and subobjectives can often be very time-consuming. In many large organizations, however, this work has already been done and the systems designer merely needs to have access to the relevant information. If it has not been done, the systems designer must initiate a process in which the objectives and subobjectives of all levels of the organization's hierarchy are defined and agreed upon. This can require much discussion and will only be successful if it has the complete support of top management.

The classic approach to definition of an organization's hierarchy of objectives is the method known as management by objectives (MBO). This method proceeds by first having top management define a number of long-term strategic objectives. These are refined by the subordinate levels of the organization into subobjectives or goals, the achievement of which will result in the accomplishment of the strategic objectives. This process generally involves much discussion in order to coordinate the plans of the

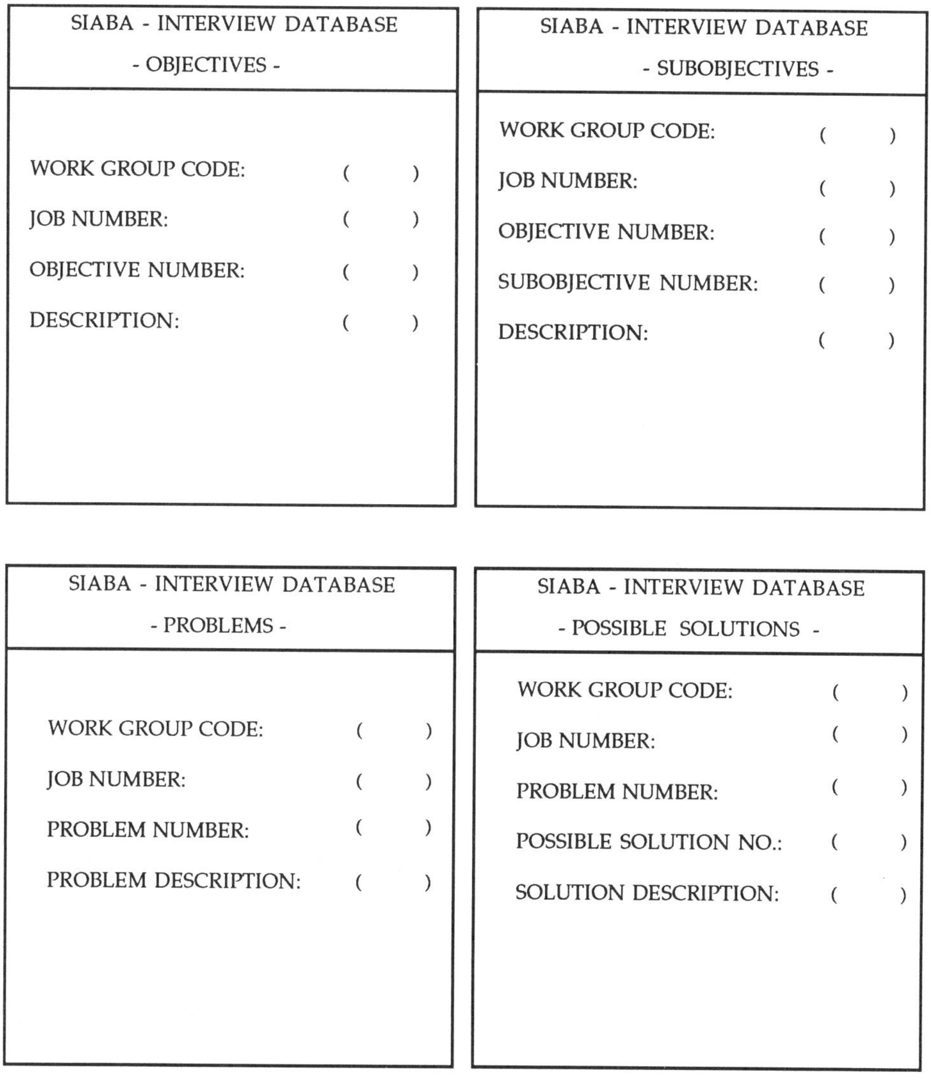

| SIABA - INTERVIEW DATABASE |
| - OBJECTIVES - |

WORK GROUP CODE:	(	)
JOB NUMBER:	(	)
OBJECTIVE NUMBER:	(	)
DESCRIPTION:	(	)

| SIABA - INTERVIEW DATABASE |
| - SUBOBJECTIVES - |

WORK GROUP CODE:	(	)
JOB NUMBER:	(	)
OBJECTIVE NUMBER:	(	)
SUBOBJECTIVE NUMBER:	(	)
DESCRIPTION:	(	)

| SIABA - INTERVIEW DATABASE |
| - PROBLEMS - |

WORK GROUP CODE:	(	)
JOB NUMBER:	(	)
PROBLEM NUMBER:	(	)
PROBLEM DESCRIPTION:	(	)

| SIABA - INTERVIEW DATABASE |
| - POSSIBLE SOLUTIONS - |

WORK GROUP CODE:	(	)
JOB NUMBER:	(	)
PROBLEM NUMBER:	(	)
POSSIBLE SOLUTION NO.:	(	)
SOLUTION DESCRIPTION:	(	)

Figure 2.13: Screens for recording objectives, subobjectives
problems and possible solutions

various levels of the organizational hierarchy. Many methods exist to aid
in reaching the necessary consensus, such as the Delphi method and the
nominal group technique.[3] The group design methods presented in
Chapter 7 can also be very useful in this regard. In the course of these

Table 2.5: Steps of the structured analysis of the current system

Steps	Files to be updated
• Determining the structure and objectives of the organization	Enterprise file, division file, department file, section file work group file, job file, problems file, possible solutions file, objectives file, subobjectives file
• Identification of the critical work groups	
• Development of the interview list for the survey of office procedures	
• Training the interview partners	
• Conducting the interviews	Task file, work step file, work step rule file, document file, task-document relationship file, problems file, possible solutions file, objectives file, subobjectives file, document flow file, source document file
• Print out of the preliminary study of the current system, discussion and revision of the survey data	Task file, work step file, work step rule file, document file, task-document relationship file, problems file, possible solutions file, objectives file, subobjectives file, document flow file, source document file
• Estimating potential benefits	Task file
• Selection of the critical cocuments with the help of the ABC analysis of information flows and the ABC analysis of potential benefits	Document file
• Analysis and decomposition of the critical documents	Data element file, source element file, data element rule file
• Print out of the final version of the study	

discussions problems will become apparent that have to be solved before the objectives can be met. In order to solve these problems, short- and medium-term subobjectives will have to be formulated. Subobjectives on this level should be concrete with explicit target dates by when they must be accomplished. It must be possible to assess the degree of accomplishment by the examination of easily measured, tangible results. Consider, for example, a medium-sized company that has set itself the objective of doubling its market share in five years. From that the production department might derive the subobjective of doubling the volume of production. That, however, might require that a production planning and control (PPC) system be installed to cope with the expanded level of operations. Assume that the installation of the PPC system would have to happen before the end of the current year in order to gear up production in time to meet the plan. In this case the installation of the PPC system is a concrete subobjective with an easily measurable result that has to be accomplished before a specific target date. This example shows how MBO helps to develop a plan which coordinates activities on different levels of the organizational hierarchy. In addition MBO tends to improve employee motivation by involving the different levels of the organization in the planning process and to provide a consistent basis for the evaluation and control of employees and work groups.

The results of the MBO process are stored in the interview database in the objectives file, the subobjectives file, the problems file and the possible solutions file. This information always relates to a specific employee, usually a division, department or section manager. The contents of the four files will often exhibit multiple relationships. In the example the subobjective of the installation of the PPC system will be recorded by one record in the subobjectives file. Achieving such a subobjective by the end of the current year would undoubtedly generate numerous problems such as the selection of an appropriate PPC system, training the employees involved, etc. These would be recorded in the problems file. Candidate PPC systems might be stored in the possible solutions file. In this way an entry in one of the four files can eventually result in entries in the others.

Identification of the Critical Work Groups

The information stored in these four files provides the basis for the second step in the structured analysis of the current system, the identification of the those work groups which must be examined in detail. The selection of the critical work groups involves a number of considerations. The simplest case occurs when, as in the above example, someone has formulated the subobjective of the installation of a specific information system. In this case all groups which will be affected by the planned information system must be investigated. The selection process becomes more complex if the procedure for the identification of the critical work groups has to be derived from the problems discovered in the initial interviews. In that case it is first necessary to identify the subset of problems which can be solved through the provision of information resources. Then a rough data model is formulated which could provide those resources. After that those work groups are selected which would provide input for or use output from the data model. These work groups will have to be analyzed in detail. Another approach to the identification of the critical work groups involves the selection of the groups which perform particularly labour-intensive tasks. The labour-intensity of such tasks will probably be reflected in the contents of the problems file. These work groups also belong on the list of critical work groups which need to be analyzed in detail.

Development of the Interview List for the Survey of Office Procedures

Once the list of critical work groups has been compiled, it is possible to proceed to the third step of the structured analysis of the current system, the development of the interview list for the survey of office procedures. This list contains the names of the individual employees whose jobs are to be analyzed. It is important here to ensure that a good cross-section of the employees of each critical work group is selected. If several employees perform exactly the same tasks, it is only necessary to interview one typical example. That is only acceptable, however, if the jobs are really identical. If that is not the case, the organization is running the risk that the information system evolved from the results of the analysis will not address all existing problems.

Training the Interview Partners

The fourth step of the structured analysis of the current system consists in the preparation of the interview partners. This is best accomplished through a short presentation by the systems designer who will be interviewing the participants. The purpose of the presentation is to give the interviewees a clear picture of the kinds of information that will be solicited so that the interviews can be held as efficiently as possible. As aids in the presentation the systems designer should show examples of the job-task-document matrix, the list of procedure steps per task, the physical and logical information flows, the list of problems and possible solutions as well as the list of objectives and subobjectives. The importance of each of these documents should be explained to the interview partners. In addition, the interview partners should be asked to have examples available of each document used to accomplish their tasks. It should be stressed that these examples ought to contain real data, because empty forms are usually not informative enough. If there are variations of the different documents, then an example of each variation should be solicited. It must be made clear to the interview partners that the systems designer needs a comprehensive overview of the multiplicity of data associated with each job. This is extremely important, because most mistakes in systems design result from misapprehensions about data relationships.

Care should be taken that the preparation of the interview partners be carried out in an unthreatening atmosphere of friendly cooperation. The interview partners should not get the feeling that they are being evaluated, but rather that their active assistance is being sought in order to improve procedures in a creative and participative fashion. The interviewer should avoid remarks that might be perceived by the job holder as a criticism. The successful interviewer makes an impression of kindness and sympathy and expresses genuine concern for the problems of the jobs. Under no circumstances should the interviewee have reason to suspect that his or her job is going to be eliminated or altered in some negative way.

Conducting the Interviews

The behavioural guidelines given above are also important for the fifth step of the structured analysis of the current system, the conducting of the interviews. Here as well qualities such as patience and empathy are prerequisites for success. The information to be solicited in the interviews is shown in the screens for the maintenance of the interview database. It is important, however, that these screens not be used in an overly formulistic manner as though they were questionnaires to be filled out. It is also usually not a good idea to put the interview results in a laptop computer during the interviews. Such behaviour will often be interpreted by the interviewee as threatening, superficial or confusing. The systems designer should strive rather to have a real conversation with the interviewee, to listen carefully and to interact with the material presented. The interviewer should take handwritten notes which are then analyzed, sorted out and recorded **after** the interview. The documents provided by the interviewee should be systematically logged and filed together with the notes taken.

Discussion of the Survey Data

The results of each interview should be recorded in the interview data base as soon as possible. At that point a preliminary version of the survey data should be printed out which includes the reports shown in Table 2.6. These data should then be discussed one more time with the interviewee in a second interview in order to guarantee completeness and accuracy. Any inaccuracies should then be corrected and missing data supplemented in the interview database.

Estimating Benefits

After all interview data have been surveyed in the manner described above, it is possible to begin thinking about the potential benefits of a new or improved system. This should be done only after all data have been gathered so that one is better able to envision a comprehensive solution. It is important to avoid seeing jobs as isolated phenomena, but rather to consider them as components of one integrated totality. On the basis of a

Table 2.6: Preliminary version of the study of the current system

- Job-task-document matrix

- List of the work steps per task

- List of the work step rules

- Physical information flows

- Logical information flows

- List of objectives and subobjectives

- List of problems and possible solutions

better understanding of the total system enriched by the information gathered in the interviews the systems designer can then estimate the potential improvements for each task and store these data in the task file. There are two sources of these kinds of benefits, the reduction of clerical work and the improvement of planning and control.

In the SIABA model the potential benefit through reduction of clerical work is expressed as a percentage of the time needed for each task. In this case the systems designer estimates the percentage amount by which the time for each task could be reduced if data processing resources were applied in an optimal fashion. The list of work steps per task can be used as an aid in making this calculation. Savings are frequently achievable by eliminating work steps. It is possible, however, that the new system requires new work steps that were not necessary in the old system. For this reason it is necessary to compare the total number of work steps per task in both the new and the old systems. The potential benefit can thus be estimated by the following formula:

$$\text{potential benefit as \%} = \frac{\text{number of work steps in new system}}{\text{number of work steps in old system}}$$

This percentage is input in the task screen in the field, 'POTENTIAL TIME REDUCTION'.

The second possibility for achieving benefits has to do with improvements in planning and control. In most cases this type of benefit is much more significant than savings resulting from the elimination of clerical work. The benefits of improved planning and control come from having a better basis for decision making. The availability of a more scientific basis for decision making increases the probability that a given decision will be the optimal one. Certain techniques from statistical decision theory can be used to quantify these kinds of benefits. The most important concept here is the idea of expected value. Expected value represents the long-term average outcome of a decision and can best be understood by considering an example.

Assume that the business of a consulting company consists in providing temporary technical staff to large concerns. The company uses freelance subcontractors to perform this service. Each subcontractor costs $14,200 a month and brings in revenues of $17,040. The consulting company must, however, reserve the capacity of its subcontractors before the clients have committed themselves. That means that each reserved but unused consultant costs the company $14,200 per month. For simplicity's sake it is assumed that the demand is always for ten, eleven, twelve or thirteen freelance consultants per month. An analysis of the demand of the last sixty months showed the frequency distribution given in Table 2.7A. These frequencies can be considered to represent the probabilities of future demand if one believes that no significant changes are going to happen in this business environment. Table 2.7B shows the monetary results in terms of net revenue per month of all combinations of possible decisions and actual demand. If, for example, twelve freelance consultants are reserved for a particular month in which the demand turns out to be for only eleven consultants, the net revenue will be $17,040 ((11 x $17,040) - (12 x $14,200)). Every decision has an expected value which is calculated by the multiplication of each possible monetary outcome by the probability of that outcome and the subsequent addition of those products. The expected value expresses the long-term average net revenue which one can expect to

Table 2.7: Example of statistical decision theory

Table 2.7A: Frequency distribution

Demand for consultants	Number of months with this demand	Frequency distribution
10	6	10 %
11	18	30 %
12	30	50 %
13	6	10 %

Table 2.7B: Monetary results of the various decision possibilities

Actual demand	Number of consultants reserved			
	10	11	12	13
10	$ 28,400	$ 14,200	0	- $ 14,200
11	$ 28,400	$ 31,240	$ 17,040	$ 2,840
12	$ 28,400	$ 31,240	$ 34,080	$ 19,880
13	$ 28,400	$ 31,240	$ 34,080	$ 36,920

Table 2.7C: Expected values

Actual demand	Probability	Number of reserved consultants			
		10	11	12	13
10	10%	$ 2,840	$ 1,420	0	- $ 1,420
11	30%	$ 8,520	$ 9,372	$ 5,112	$ 852
12	50%	$ 14,200	$ 15,620	$ 17,040	$ 9,940
13	10%	$ 2,840	$ 3,124	$ 3,408	$ 3,692
		$ 28,400	$ 29,536	$ 25,560	$ 13,064

Average = $ 24,140   ↑___ optimal decision

Table 2.7D: Expected values with perfect information

Actual demand	Probability	Result with perfect prediction	Expected value
10	10 %	$ 28,400	$ 2,840
11	30 %	$ 31,240	$ 9,372
12	50 %	$ 34,080	$ 17,040
13	10 %	$ 36,920	$ 3,692
Expected profit			$ 32,944
Expected value of perfect information			$ 3,408

attain with a particular decision. The expected values for this example are given in Table 2.7C and show quite conclusively that with the given probability distribution the optimal decision under conditions of uncertainty is to reserve eleven consultants since this decision has the highest expected value.

Another important concept from statistical decision theory is the idea of expected profit with perfect prediction. This value expresses the long-term average net revenue if an instrument for the perfect prediction of future demand is available. This value minus the expected value of the optimal decision under conditions of uncertainty yields the expected value of perfect information, as illustrated in Table 2.7D. These expected values set the limits for possible improvements of planning and control in a particular decision situation. In the example the average expected value of $24,140 per month (random decision-making) can be raised to $29,536 through the use of the statistical decision model and to $32,944 through the use of a perfect predictor of future demand. That means that the maximum value of additional information in this decision situation can never be more than $8,804 ($32,944 - $24,140). It is important to note here that the value of information is never unlimited but rather always determined by the monetary outcomes of the various possible decisions and the probabilities of those outcomes. The concept of expected value should, therefore, always be applied when estimating the possible benefits of improved planning and control.

Empirical studies have shown that the most important possibilities for attaining benefits in industrial environments lie in three areas:[4]

1. Planning and control of the distribution of finished products.

2. Planning and control of the use of material, machines and labour in manufacturing.

3. Planning and control of procurement.

The possible benefits result from the reduction of the time needed for various activities, the reduction of the effort needed to achieve a particular result, the increase of the result attained with a given effort and the improved coordination of activities. Many powerful quantitative techniques exist such as linear and non-linear programming, queuing theory, mathematical inventory models, etc., which can be used in combination with information systems to achieve quite remarkable increases in efficiency. In order to quantify these increases it is necessary to examine the way decisions are being made, noting the most important quantitative characteristics of each decision. These characteristics might include such things as the value of inventories, machine capacities, material and labour requirements per unit of production, etc. Once this is done, it is possible to develop a new strategy for improved decision-making by constructing a quantitative model of the decision process.

On the basis of the model and the statistics of past performance, a good estimate of the quantifiable benefits of the new strategy can usually be made. This estimate should then be stored in the task file of the SIABA database in the field, 'POSSIBLE BENEFIT THROUGH IMPROVEMENT OF PLANNING AND CONTROL'.

Selection of the Critical Information Flows
After all the benefits have been estimated, the critical information flows are selected on the basis of two quantitative analyses. Both analyses use the technique of the ABC classification. The ABC classification is a reliable way to determine which of a large number of items is the most important. The method is borrowed from the science of inventory control where it is used to classify the items in an inventory. The first step is to find out the monetary value of the yearly turnover of each item. Then all items are listed in descending sequence of that value. In each line appear the monetary value of yearly turnover for the given article, the yearly turnover in number of items and the cumulative figures for turnover value and number of items including all previously listed items. The cumulative figures are expressed as percentages of the total turnover value and total number of items. It turns out in almost all inventories that the

most important 10 per cent of the items (the so-called A items) make up about 70 per cent of the total value of yearly turnover. The most important 30 per cent of the items account for about 90 per cent of the total value of turnover while roughly 70 per cent of the items correspond to only 10 per cent of the total turnover value. These relationships are illustrated in Fig. 2.14. The obvious conclusion is that to achieve efficient inventory control, it is appropriate to concentrate primarily on the A items. The ABC classification can be applied with great utility to the analysis of both information flows and potential benefits. An ABC analysis of potential benefits is shown in Table 2.8. Instead of inventory items, tasks are analyzed. In order to do this it is first necessary to calculate the total quantifiable benefits per task by using the following formula:

total benefits per task=(task as percentage of total job x yearly costs of job
x percentage potential time reduction)
+ quantifiable benefit of improvement of
planning and control

Then the tasks are listed in descending sequence of benefits per task and the cumulative amounts calculated. In the example there are four tasks, each of which accounts for 25 per cent of the total number of tasks. The analysis indicates that the first 25 per cent of the tasks provide 51 per cent of the total potential benefits, the first 50 per cent about 72 per cent and so on. The typically skewed distribution aids the identification of those tasks which should receive particular attention in the planning of the new information system. In this simple example this would be clear even without an ABC analysis. In practice, however, there are often hundreds or even thousands of tasks to be considered, and without a powerful analytical instrument, priorities must frequently be set in an arbitrary fashion.

A second application of the ABC classification has to do with information flows and is illustrated in Table 2.9. In this case each information flow or document is weighted by the monetary value of the labour associated with it. The weight is calculated by a proportional

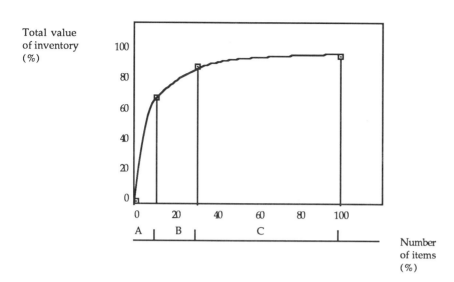

Figure: 2.14: ABC classification in inventory control

allocation of the yearly costs of all jobs that work with that information flow. The ABC analysis shown in the example is implied by the job-task-document matrix of Fig. 2.3 if the yearly costs of jobs 1, 2, 3 and 4 are assumed to be $20,000, $30,000, $40,000 and $50,000 respectively. First the yearly costs of each job are allocated to the tasks on the basis of the percentage of the total job that each task represents. These amounts are in turn allocated to the documents that are needed to perform the tasks. For each document the cost allocations from all tasks are summed to yield a total cost allocation per document. This value is then used to sort the documents in descending sequence and compute the ABC classification. This form of the ABC analysis is a measurement of how widely used a given document is in the organization. Widely used information flows receive high weightings because these weightings include cost allocations from many different jobs. Such information flows are very important with regard to systems integration and are usually prime candidates for inclusion in centralized databases. It is precisely information flows of this type that connect the various functions of an organization and, therefore,

Table 2.8: ABC analysis of potential benefits

Task/ job	Potential benefit	Cumulative benefits	Cum. % of total benefits	% of tasks
1/2	12,000	12,000	51	25
1/1	5,000	17,000	72	50
1/3	4,000	21,000	89	75
1/4	2,500	23,500	100	100

provide the best opportunities for the synergetic benefits of an integrated information system.

With the help of the ABC analysis of potential benefits and the ABC analysis of information flows it is possible to identify the critical information flows. The critical information flows are those that are involved in tasks with a high benefits potential and those that are used by many jobs. These two sets of information will typically have many overlaps. The most important 20 per cent in both analyses are almost certainly critical. How many more information flows should be included in the critical list depends on the estimated cost of the planned system. Normally the greater the number of information flows included in the system, the more expensive the system becomes. The marginal costs of information systems development should not exceed the marginal benefits. At this stage the relationship between marginal costs and benefits can only be roughly approximated, but that is usually sufficient to recognize the most important priorities.

It is useful to set a flag in those records of the document file which correspond to critical documents. This is accomplished with the critical document code (CDC). If a document is critical, then this field contains an

Table 2.9: ABC analysis of information flows

Doc.	Weighting by salary costs	Cumulative weighting	Cum. % of salary costs	% of documents
A	85,000	85,000	61	25
B	24,000	109,000	79	50
C	21,000	130,000	93	75
D	10,000	140,000	100	100

'X', otherwise it is blank. The critical document code can be set manually or automatically. Manual setting is done with the maintenance program for the document file. Automatic setting is carried out by the programs which perform the ABC analyses.

Automatic setting of the critical document code involves inputting a parameter, n, when performing ABC analyses. This parameter indicates the percentage of the tasks or documents as seen from the beginning of the descending list which are to be considered critical. After performing the analysis the program sets the critical document code in all document records that are associated with the top n per cent of the tasks or information flows depending on the type of analysis. This flag then enables the automatic generation of a list of critical documents which is consistent with the results of the ABC analyses.

Analysis of the Critical Documents
With the aid of the ABC analyses and the rough estimates of costs and benefits, the systems designer finalizes the list of critical documents. These documents, together with the corresponding source documents, represent the raw material out of which the new information system will be fashioned and must, therefore, be analyzed in more detail. Each document

consists of a certain number of data elements. Each data element has certain characteristics such as length and type (i.e. numeric or alphanumeric). The data elements also are often structured in some way. All this information must be solicited and stored in the appropriate files of the interview database. Storing this kind of information requires a set of conventions. The SIABA convention is borrowed from the Cobol programming language. A five-digit alphanumeric field, for example, has the Cobol description, 'XXXXX', a six-digit amount field with two digits to the right of the decimal looks like this: '9999.99'. Often data elements are subdivided into other data elements. This is indicated by a number showing the group level; a group level with a lower number includes all immediately following group levels with a higher number. The following syntax defines the data elements needed for storing a name:

Data element name: Name
Group level..............:   01

Data element name: Family name
Group level..............:   02
Cobol picture............:   X(30)

Data element name: First name
Group level..............:   02
Cobol picture............:   X(20)

This means that a data element, 'Name', exists which is subdivided into two other data elements   'Family name' and 'First name'. The information is stored as three records in the data element file. Since up to ninety-nine group levels can be defined, any plausible data structure can be represented. Another convention borrowed from Cobol is the OCCURS parameter. In some documents there are series of fields that have identical characteristics. Instead of storing separate records for each element it is easier just to set the OCCURS parameter.

A convention which does not come from the Cobol language is the key field indicator. If the data element is an important sorting and selection criterion for the document, then this field is set to 'X'. That means that the other data elements of the document are dependent on this field in some way. If the data content of the document is stored on magnetic media, such fields usually become keys. At this stage it is often not yet clear which data elements will become keys. If it is known already, however, then the key field indicator should be set.

The values that a given data element can take on are often limited by some sort of validation rule. In the case of a six-digit numeric date, for example, only those numbers are valid which represent a valid date. In other cases values must belong to a specific of values stored in a validation table. These kinds of validation rules (e.g. 'valid date' or 'see table of valid entries') should also be stored as a text field in the data element file.

After determining the characteristics of a data element the systems designer must find out if the data element is derived from any other data elements (source elements). If that is the case, then the source elements should be recorded in the source element file and the derivation rule in the source element rule file. It is possible that the source elements are in the same document or in other documents (source documents).

The conventions described above enable rigorous descriptions of all data elements. These descriptions are critically important both for database and program design. Most of the errors in systems design are traceable back to an inadequate understanding of the data elements involved. For this reason it is important to perform this part of the study of the current system with meticulous care and thoroughness.

Printing Out the Study of the Current System

The last step in the study of the current system is the printing out of the final report which consists of the components shown in Table 2.10. This collection of information gives the systems designer everything he or she needs to know in order to define a prototype information system. The structured approach to the analysis of the current system guarantees that the prototype will include the most important information flows. In

Table 2.10: Final version of the study of the current system

- Job-task-document matrix

- List of the work steps per task

- List of the work step rules

- Physical information flows

- Logical information flows

- List of objectives and subobjectives

- List of problems and possible solutions

- ABC analysis of potential benefits

- ABC analysis of information flows

- List of critical documents

- List of documents with data elements

- List of data elements, source elements and rules

addition the database developed in the course of the project provides a rich source of data for further analyses. Many useful graphics such as organization charts, objectives' trees and functional decompositions can be generated on the basis of these data. Such products help the project participants to understand better how the organization functions and how it could be improved. Once an enterprise model in the form of a SIABA database is available, a dynamic feedback process can be initiated which leads to a continuous increase in efficiency.

2.3 Review Questions and Exercises

1. Why does it make sense to develop an enterprise model?

2. What kinds of information should be included in an enterprise model?

3. What strategic information should be included in an enterprise model?

4. What operational information should be included in an enterprise model?

5. Name the most important aspects of the structured interview technique in developing an enterprise model.

6. What advantages can be had by storing the enterprise model as a database?

7. Discuss the two kinds of benefits provided by information systems and how these can be estimated. Which is usually the more important?

8. Discuss how the critical documents of an organization can be determined.

2.4 Notes

[1] The name SIABA is derived from the German *System für Ist-Aufnahme und Bedarfsanalyse* which means system for organization study and requirements analysis.

[2] Pseudocode is a method for representing the basic constructs of structured programming in simple English. Logical conditions and repeating loops are indicated by keywords such as IF and WHILE.

[3] The Delphi method and the nominal group technique are forecasting techniques based on the querying of experts. With the Delphi method the experts are queried in isolation from each other using questionnaires. With the nominal group technique the experts interact in a structured meeting.

In both cases the experts can revise their opinions on the basis of feedback from the group.

[4]R. G. Murdock and J. E. Ross, *Information Systems for Modern Management*, Englewood Cliffs, NJ: Prentice Hall, 1975, p. 253.

3 Standardizing the Components of Software Systems

3.1 The Main Functions of Software Systems

All commercial software systems have two basic functions, the storage and manipulation of data. These functions are carried out by computer programs which record the data in some convenient format and display these data in a manner useful for the support of particular human activities. Many different kinds of techniques such as database management systems, various programming languages, etc., are employed to accomplish these ends. These techniques can all be reduced, however, to a few basic constructs. All commercial software systems maintain three categories of files using three categories of programs.

The three different types of programs can be constructed in a great variety of ways. Such variety, however, adds little to the business utility of software systems. If, on the other hand, the programs in a given data processing installation are limited to a few standardized building blocks, quite remarkable gains in the efficiency of software development can be achieved. Standardized program modules are easier to use and cheaper to maintain. For this reason overall software productivity depends a great deal on the degree of standardization of software modules. This chapter presents some suggestions for the standardization of the three categories of programs and describes how they can be used to process the three categories of files. These suggestions are meant to show only one of the many ways to approach the problem of module standardization. The precise details of implementation depend on the processing platforms available in a particular organization and the types of processing typically required.

3.1.1 The Three Categories of Files

The characteristics of files and databases play an eminent role in systems development because of the critical importance of data access times in modern software systems. In today's software it is usually necessary to have direct access to the data by one or more keys in order to get to the desired records with as few reads as possible. Data access by logical key values requires, however, the storage of additional data (sometimes called structure data) to support the rapid retrieval of information. The more key fields desired, the more structure data must be stored, the maintenance of which reduces the overall speed of the file management system. That means that adding additional keys will at some point involve diminishing returns as regards overall systems performance because the structure data have to be updated every time a new record is stored. The systems designer must, therefore, consider the tradeoffs involved and arrive at a reasonable compromise between the number of logical keys and the desired access speeds for various types of information.

One way to achieve this compromise involves considering the files of an application system as belonging to one of three categories:

1. Applications files. These are the main repositories of user data, e.g. the master files of an accounting system.
2. Table files. These files contain lists of valid values, e.g. lists of valid accounting codes, lists of valid project codes. Table data are used to validate or supplement user data or to provide parameters for some kind of processing.

3. Activity files.   Activity files are used to facilitate the operation of
                        software systems. One use of activity files is to pass
                        data between two programs that do not run
                        concurrently. Another is to reformat and/or to sort
                        the data into a different sequence. Such a facility
                        reduces the number of keys needed in the application
                        files. Activity data are of a more transient nature
                        than applications or table data.

Many different kinds of data structures can be used to store the three
categories of user data. The only essential thing is that keyed access by at
least one key is possible.

Applications files are normally organized according to the business
area they concern. For example, there are inventory master files, personnel
master files, supplier master files, etc. An applications system will usually
consist of numerous applications files that have multiple relationships
with each other. In any given system, however, there should not be more
than **one table file** and **one activity file**. Each of these files need have only a
single key. This simple structure is made possible by having a generalized
record layout consisting of a key portion and a data portion. Both the key
portion and the data portion can be subdivided into as many different
fields as needed within the given lengths. In this way it is possible to store
many different record types easily in the same file.

The usefulness of this threefold file organization is illustrated with
the example of a central table file. A typical table in an applications system
has a search field (sometimes called an argument) and usually one or more
data fields (also known as the function). In Table 3.1 two examples of tables
are shown. The first is a table of accounting codes from an accounting
system. The search argument is the two-digit accounting code, the function
consists of the account numbers that are used for debits and credits
associated with that code. This table might be used, for example, to generate
the proper postings for different kinds of business transactions. Each
transaction in this case would contain an accounting code. The program
would read each transaction and use the accounting code contained therein

Table 3.1: Examples of tables

Table example A

Account as a function of accounting code

Argument	----------------Function----------------	
Accounting code	Debit account	Credit account
01	01504712	01507712
02	01504711	01507711
03	01504710	01507710
04	01504709	01507709
05	01504708	01507708

Table example B

Discount rate as a function of customer number

Argument	Function
Customer number	Discount rate
50001234	2.5
50004545	0.0
50001007	5.0
50001605	4.3

to find the appropriate entry in the table. This information could then be used to produce the required bookkeeping entries. The second table example shows discounts which depend on an eight-digit customer code. In this example each customer has a particular discount percentage. An invoicing program might use this table to calculate the discount amount for the invoice.

These kinds of tables can be easily handled by one central table file. Every record in the file must have the layout shown in Table 3.2. Each

Table 3.2: Example of a central table file

	Composite key		
Tab. ID Col. 1-3	Application key Columns 4 - 24	Valid from date Columns 25 - 28	Function fields Columns 29 - 500
BSC	01	890703	0150471201507712
BSC	02	890703	0150471101507711
BSC	03	890703	0150471001507710
BSC	04	890703	0150470901507709
BSC	05	890703	0150470801507708
KRB	50001234	890703	25
KRB	50004545	890703	00
KRB	50001007	890703	50
KRB	50001605	890703	43

different table is uniquely identified by a three-digit alphanumeric code (table ID) which occupies the first position of the key of every record in the file. The next part of the key contains the argument of the given table. Unneeded space in this part of the key is padded out to the right with blanks. The third portion of the record (in this case columns 25 to 28) contains the date when the table entry becomes valid. By arranging the table ID, the key and the validity date in this fashion it becomes possible to retrieve the table data easily and directly from the table file in the proper logical sequence. In this way all the tables of an organization can be maintained in a single physical file. The field lengths used in Table 3.2 are not the only ones possible, but have been found to be adequate for most practical situations.

A similar strategy can be applied to the activity file. Activity files are used primarily for two purposes:

1. Message transfer. In order to pass messages from one program to a second program which is not active at the same time, the first program stores a message in the activity file which is later read by the second program. This facility is used most frequently by online programs which

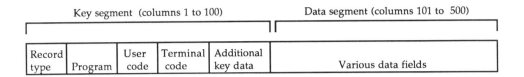

Figure 3.1: Record layout for activity file

store requests for batch processes involving too much
data to run in online mode.

2. Sorting.   In order to sort selected records from one or more
applications files, the records are written to the
activity file and read back out again. With this
technique it is possible to arrange the data into a
sequence which does not correspond to any key in the
applications files. By doing this one avoids the
necessity of having to have a key for every
conceivable sequence needed by the application. This
method is particularly appropriate if the data sequence
in question is needed by only one program in the
system, involves only a subset of the records of the
application file but, because of unpredictable data
volumes, cannot be handled by an internal sort. In
such cases it would be inadvisable to add an
additional key because the maintenance of the
structure data would create overheads for the entire
system while the benefit would be limited to only a
small part.

As illustrated in Fig. 3.1 the records of the activity file are segmented
into a key portion and a data portion analogous to the structure of the
central table file. The key portion, however, must be considerably larger
than in the case of the table file because it is sometimes necessary to

concatenate many fields in order to achieve the desired result. The key always has two portions, each of which can be subdivided into several fields. The first part identifies the logical file within the physical activity file and is the same for all records of the logical file. In interactive applications this part should contain a record type, program identification, user identification and terminal code so that many different users can use the file at the same time without running the risk of corrupting each other's data. In the case of batch applications, user identifications and terminal codes are usually not relevant so that other conventions must be adopted to ensure the proper segregation of record types (logical files). It is essential that these conventions be controlled centrally by a data administrator to guarantee the integrity of the activity file. The second part of the key and the entire data portion can be freely formatted by the applications program. When the activity file is used for sorting or manipulating data, the records are usually deleted at the end of the processing by the program that created them. When the activity file is used to pass data to batch processes, the records are either deleted by the batch process or by a maintenance process that runs at certain intervals (e.g. once a week).

3.1.2 The Three Categories of Programs

All required processing of the three categories of user data can be accomplished by three categories of programs:

1. Database maintenance programs.   These types of programs are used to retrieve, display, insert, alter and delete records from files.

2. List generators.   These programs are used to list data from files on a screen or printer.

3. Transformation programs.　These programs copy data from one or more files into one or more files and transform those data in some fashion. A program which updates a master file is a typical example of a transformation program.

In the next section of this chapter the basic variations of these three program categories are described. Twelve basic archetypes or program clichés will be defined which can be used to construct practically any business software system required.

3.2 The Twelve Basic Types of Applications

3.2.1 General Characteristics of Database Maintenance Programs

Interactive database maintenance programs read, store and delete data. They should also be able to scroll backwards and forwards through the data in the sequence of a logical key. In addition a number of ancillary functions are very useful to complement the main functions. In summary the following functions should be available in all interactive database maintenance programs:

1. Fetch.　A key value is input into a screen field which causes the program to access the appropriate record and display it on the screen.

2. Scroll forward.　The next record or records in the sequence of the logical key are accessed and displayed on the screen.

3. Scroll backward.　The previous record or records in the sequence of the logical key are accessed and displayed on the screen.

4. Insert.   A new record is input on the screen and added to
                              the file.

5. Alter.   An existing record is read in from the file, displayed
                              on the screen, changed by the user and rewritten to
                              the file.

6. Delete.   An existing record is deleted from the file.

7. Prepare screen.   All processing having to do with the supple-
                              mentation, editing and checking of the data
                              displayed on the screen is executed.

8. Help function.   A description of the current function and directions
                              for its use are displayed on the screen.

9. Table view.   For screen fields, the valid entries for which are
                              stored in tables, it should be possible in most cases to
                              display a scrollable window of the contents of the
                              table and to select one of the entries for the input
                              field. An exception to this is the case of sensitive
                              data where the user is not allowed access to all
                              possible values for the field.

10. End of processing.   This function causes the program to end its
                              processing and return control to the calling
                              program.

These ten program functions are initiated through the input of some sort of control information. There are three common methods to accomplish this:

1. Each function has a code which is input in a certain position on the screen. This code in combination with the return or data entry key causes the desired action to be performed.

2. Each function is assigned to a program function key (PF key), the pressing of which causes the chosen action to be performed.

3. The various functions are listed in selection lists which appear when the cursor is positioned at a certain place in the screen and the return or data entry key is pressed. The cursor is positioned again within each list to indicate the desired choice and the return or data entry key is pressed again. Moving the cursor to a selection usually causes that selection to be highlighted in some way. This type of selection list is sometimes called a pull-down menu.

The first two methods, singly or in combination, are used in most large computer systems. The third method is found primarily in single-user systems because the interaction required between screen and processor normally creates too much of a burden for multi-user systems. In the examples described below the first two methods are employed. The function keys used correspond to the ten functions described above.

3.2.2 Database Maintenance Program: One Screen = One Record

The first basic type of application is shown in Fig. 3.2. In this example a file is maintained one record at a time by an interactive program. The screen contains a formatted layout of the record. In order to read a record from the file a key, in this case the personnel number, is entered in the appropriate field, and the PF1 key (Fetch) is pressed. The program then reads the record from the file and displays the contents on the screen. The user can change the data fields by typing over the original contents and pressing the PF5 key (Alter). If a record with the given key is not available in the file, the user can enter the entire record and store it by pressing the PF4 key

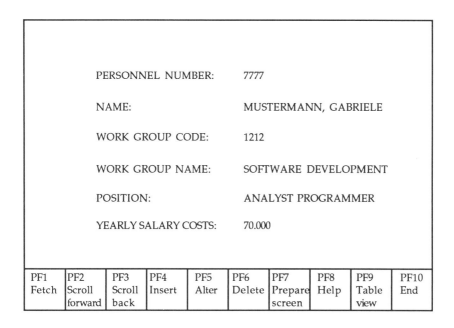

PERSONNEL NUMBER: 7777

NAME: MUSTERMANN, GABRIELE

WORK GROUP CODE: 1212

WORK GROUP NAME: SOFTWARE DEVELOPMENT

POSITION: ANALYST PROGRAMMER

YEARLY SALARY COSTS: 70.000

PF1	PF2	PF3	PF4	PF5	PF6	PF7	PF8	PF9	PF10
Fetch	Scroll forward	Scroll back	Insert	Alter	Delete	Prepare screen	Help	Table view	End

Figure 3.2:   Screen layout for a
                    database maintenance program,
                    one screen = one record

(Insert). When deleting records the user proceeds in a way similar to altering. The key value is input and the PF1 key is pressed. The record appears on the screen. The deletion is then requested by pressing the PF6 key. It is a good idea to force the user to confirm the delete request by pressing the PF6 key a second time. These four PF keys handle all basic database maintenance functions.

In addition there are a few more functions that greatly increase the utility of this kind of application. For example, it is often very useful to be able to scroll backward and forward through the data in the logical sequence of the main key. This is accomplished by the PF2 and PF3 keys. By pressing the PF2 key (Forward) the user accesses the record with the next higher key value. The PF3 key (Backward) causes the display of the record with the next lower key value. By repeated use of these keys the user can scroll backward and forward through the file as desired. Another function that is normally needed is the preparation and/or checking of the input fields. In Fig. 3.2, for example, the field 'Work group code' has to be verified against a table of valid entries. The same table provides the name of the work group in question. Both the verification of the input as well as the accessing of the name text is caused by pressing the PF7 key (Prepare screen). This PF key is usually pressed before insertion or alteration of a record and causes all verification logic to be executed, including the checking that does not have to do with tables. This checking also happens, of course, as part of the processing associated with the PF4 (Insert) and PF5 (Alter) keys. It is often useful, however, to be able to see the results of such processing on the screen before changes are made to the database. This is particularly the case when input data are supplemented by much data from tables. In this way, by using the PF7 key the user can get some feedback about the input before it becomes permanent.

Another function that should be included in every well-designed system is the help function. This function is called up by pressing the PF8 key and causes a description of the program function to be displayed on the screen. The user can call up this function at any time to look up details about the operation of the program. A second type of help function is useful with regard to fields that are verified against tables. If one forgets the valid values for a particular field, it is possible to input a question mark in the field and press the PF9 key. A scrollable list containing entries from the table then appears on the screen. The user can scroll through the table, select one of the values and return to the main program. The selected value then appears in the field.

The user must, of course, have a way of ending the program execution. This is done by pressing the PF10 key.

This sample application contains all program functions that are needed for a modern, ergonomically sound user interface for a database maintenance program. There are, of course, many different ways to design this kind of program. The PF keys could, for example, be set up completely differently without diminishing the functionality of the program. The important thing is to establish these conventions once and for all for a given organization and then to adhere faithfully to the standard in all software development projects.

3.2.3 Database Maintenance Program: One Screen = Multiple Records

The basic model program described above is sufficient for a large number of applications. It is, however, often useful to be able to process more than one record at a time on the screen. This requires an enhanced version of the basic model such as the one illustrated in Fig. 3.3. In this case instead of displaying a single record on the screen, a scrollable list of records is displayed. The basic functions available are very similar to those of the first model program. Here as well records can be fetched, stored and deleted. Because multiple records appear on the screen, however, the PF keys as defined in the first model are not sufficient to tell the program exactly what is to be done. Some method is needed to let the program know which records of the list are to be manipulated. One way to do this is to have a function column which allows the user to specify which record or records in the list are to processed. A typical convention would be to input an I for insert, an A for alter or a D for delete in the function column next to the record to be processed. This code then causes the record appearing in that line to be inserted, altered or deleted.

The function keys then acquire a slightly different significance. When fetching using the PF1 key a key value must be entered in a header line. In the example shown in Fig. 3.3 this is the posting date. The user enters a posting date and presses PF1. A list of inventory transactions beginning at that date then appears on the screen. Scrolling using the PF2 and PF3 keys happens the same way as in the first model except that the scrolling involves a page of records instead of just a single record. The functions associated with the PF4, PF5 and PF6 keys (Insert, Alter and Delete) are no longer necessary since these actions are controlled by the letter codes, I, A and D. The functions associated with the PF7, PF8, PF9 and PF10 keys (the Prepare screen, Help, Table view and Stop functions respectively) remain unchanged. This second basic program model allows the

FETCH INVENTORY TRANSACTIONS FROM DATE: 10MAR90

FCT	POST.DATE	ITEM NUMBER	DESCRIPTION	AMOUNT	I/R
I	10MAR90	10001211	SCREWS - 6MM	0050	I
I	10MAR90	10001203	RECEPTICLES	0003	I
I	10MAR90	10001211	SCREWS - 6MM	0100	I
I	10MAR90	10001211	SCREWS - 6MM	0120	I
I	10MAR90	10001277	FITTINGS - X42	0012	R
I	10MAR90	10001277	FITTINGS - X42	0024	R
I	11MAR90	10001542	DOWELS - 8MM	0008	I
I	11MAR90	10001212	BRASS SPRING	0015	I
I	11MAR90	10001212	BRASS SPRING	0015	I
I	11MAR90	10001277	FITTINGS - X42	0012	R
I	11MAR90	10001212	BRASS SPRING	0015	R
I	11MAR90	10001211	SCREWS - 6MM	0200	R

PF1	PF2	PF3	PF4	PF5	PF6	PF7	PF8	PF9	PF10
Fetch	Scroll forward	Scroll back	Insert	Alter	Delete	Prepare screen	Help	Table view	End

Figure 3.3:   Screen layout for a
database maintenance program,
one screen = multiple records

maintainance of a screenful of similar records, thus providing a better overview of the contents of the file.

The next three basic program models provide additional ergonomic enhancements through the use of windowing techniques. These are really only variations on the themes of the first two models. In the third basic model, for example, the screen is divided into two windows, in the fourth basic model into three windows and in the fifth basic model into four windows. Each window functions like a miniature version of the whole screen. In each one a database maintenance function with one record or multiple records is provided. Within each window the functions are exactly the same as in the first two basic program models. It is, of course, possible to have programs with more than four windows. In most cases, however, this is not really necessary and makes the screen appear excessively crowded. If it becomes necessary, the programs should be

FCT	ITEM NO.	DESCRIPTION	UNIT	UNIT PRICE	AMT	TOT. PRICE
I	50001007	DISKETTES 3.5	PC	0010.00	10	100.00
I	50001605	RIBBON X12	PC	0007.00	01	7.00
I	50000046	RIBBON N47	PC	0005.00	01	5.00
I	50007777	CABLE CENT.	PC	0102.00	01	102.00

ACTIVE WINDOW: 2

INVOICE NUMBER.......: 89015
INVOICE DATE...............: 10.03.89

CUSTOMER NUMBER: 12500
CUSTOMER NAME.......: XYZ CORP.
CUSTOMER ADDRESS.: ELDRED
                   NEW YORK 12732
DISCOUNT RATE............: 5.5

PF1	PF2	PF3	PF4	PF5	PF6	PF7	PF8	PF9	PF10
Fetch	Scroll forward	Scroll back	Insert	Alter	Delete	Prepare screen	Help	Table view	End

Figure 3.4:   Screen layout for a
              database maintenance program
              with two windows

constructed so that the windows appear and disappear as required (overlay windows); at no one time should more than four windows be visible.

3.2.4 Database Maintenance Program: Two Windows

Fig. 3.4 shows a database maintenance program with two windows. In this example two files of an invoicing system are maintained simultaneously. The first file contains the header information for each invoice, the second file the individual line items. The header information is maintained in the upper window, the line items in the scrollable list in the lower window. The key for both files is the invoice number. The user inputs an invoice number and presses Pf1. The program then reads the invoice header from the first file and the corresponding line items from the second file. With just one exception everything else happens just as in the first two basic model programs. The exception has to do with the selection of the window to be processed. Function keys always relate to the entire contents of a window. With the first two basic models there is no ambiguity because in both cases there is only one window. In this basic model program, however, there are two windows. It is, therefore, necessary to let the program know in some way which window is to be processed. One simple way to accomplish this is to have a window selection field such as shown in the upper left-hand corner of the example. Inputting a '1' in this field indicates that the program should process the upper window, a '2' indicates the lower window. Depending on the input in this field the program will apply all PF key usage to the selected window. It is a good idea to highlight the selected window in some way in order to provide the user with a visual feedback about which window is currently selected.

3.2.5 Database Maintenance Program: Three Windows

A database maintenance program with three windows is shown in Fig. 3.5. The example of the invoicing system is enhanced by the addition of a window in which an order file can be maintained. The purpose of the program is the creation of invoices. It is assumed here that an order file exists which determines the contents of the invoices. The user scans the order file in the upper window and creates the invoices in the two lower windows. If an item in the order file is to be invoiced, it need merely be selected with an appropriate code to cause it to be taken over automatically into the invoice line item window.

3.2.6 Database Maintenance Program: Four Windows

Fig. 3.6 illustrates a database maintenance program with four windows. In order to take our example a step further we assume the invoicing clerk needs access to a table of rebates per customer in order to create the invoices

FCT	ORD. NO.	CUST. NO.	ITEM NO.	DESCRIPTION	UNIT	AMT	INV.
A	544287	12500	50001007	DISKETTES 3.5	PC	10	X
A	544287	12500	50001605	RIBBON X12	PC	01	X

ACTIVE WINDOW: 2   ORDER DATA

INVOICE DATA

INVOICE NO...................:   89015
INVOICE DATE...............:   10MAR90
CUSTOMER NO................:   12500
CUSTOMER NAME.........:   XYZ CORP.
CUSTOMER ADDRESS.:   ELDRED
                                           NEW YORK 12732
DISCOUNT RATE..............:   5.5

FCT	ITEM NO.	DESCRIPTION	UNIT	UNIT PRICE	AMT	TOT.PRICE
I	50001007	DISKETTES 3.5	PC	0010.00	10	100.00
I	50001605	RIBBON X12	PC	0007.00	01	7.00
I	50000046	RIBBON N47	PC	0005.00	01	5.00

PF1	PF2	PF3	PF4	PF5	PF6	PF7	PF8	PF9	PF10
Fetch	Scroll forward	Scroll back	Insert	Alter	Delete	Prepare screen	Help	Table view	End

Figure 3.5:   Screen layout for a
database maintenance program
with three windows

in an efficient manner. This is made possible by a scrollable list displayed in a fourth window.

3.2.7 Simple List Program

This is probably the simplest basic program model but one which is essential in every business software system. The records of a file are merely listed on the printer. In the process only the most trivial changes are performed on the original data. These changes might involve the following:

ACTIVE WINDOW: 2	ORDER DATA					
FCT	ORD. NO.	CUST. NO.	ITEM NO.	DESCRIPTION	UNIT	AMT INV.
A	544287	12500	50001007	DISKETTES 3.5	PC	10 X
A	544287	12500	50001605	RIBBON X12	PC	01 X

INVOICE DATA		DISCOUNT RATES	
INVOICE NO...................:	89015	FCT CUST. NO.	DISCOUNTS
INVOICE DATE...............:	10MAR90	12500	5.5
CUSTOMER NO...............:	12500	12600	2.5
CUSTOMER NAME.........:	XYZ CORP.	12700	3.0
CUSTOMER ADDRESS.:	ELDRED	12750	4.0
	NEW YORK 12732	12770	0.0
DISCOUNT RATE.............:	5.5		

FCT	ITEM NO.	DESCRIPTION	UNIT	UNIT PRICE	AMT	TOT.PRICE
I	50001007	DISKETTES 3.5	PC	0010.00	10	100.00
I	50001605	RIBBON X12	PC	0007.00	01	7.00
I	50000046	RIBBON N47	PC	0005.00	01	5.00

PF1	PF2	PF3	PF4	PF5	PF6	PF7	PF8	PF9	PF10
Fetch	Scroll forward	Scroll back	Insert	Alter	Delete	Prepare screen	Help	Table view	End

Figure 3.6:   Screen layout for a
database maintenance program
with four windows

1. The record contents are reformatted in order to produce an easily readable print image. This might mean converting binary fields to ASCIII or inserting spaces between fields.

2. Header lines or other explanatory text are added.

3. Page skips and page numbering are added.

4. Only a particular subset of the contents of the file is printed.

This application is so common that many operating systems provide parameterized utility routines which can perform such tasks without programming. Fig. 3.7 shows a systems flow chart and pseudocode logic for this type of application.

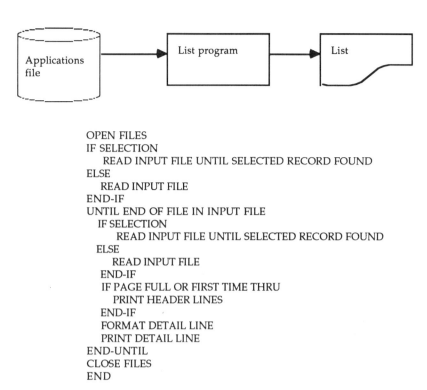

```
OPEN FILES
IF SELECTION
    READ INPUT FILE UNTIL SELECTED RECORD FOUND
ELSE
    READ INPUT FILE
END-IF
UNTIL END OF FILE IN INPUT FILE
    IF SELECTION
        READ INPUT FILE UNTIL SELECTED RECORD FOUND
    ELSE
        READ INPUT FILE
    END-IF
    IF PAGE FULL OR FIRST TIME THRU
        PRINT HEADER LINES
    END-IF
    FORMAT DETAIL LINE
    PRINT DETAIL LINE
END-UNTIL
CLOSE FILES
END
```

Figure 3.7:   Systems flow chart and processing logic
              for a simple list program

3.2.8 List Program with Sorting and Summing

Many reporting requirements cannot be met through the use of simple lists. It is often necessary to print the records in a given sequence or to create sums for all records with a particular value in a given field or fields. The sorting and the summing usually have to do with the same control fields. The sorting sequence often involves several fields. Each time one of the component fields changes, a sum of the values of a particular numeric field or fields is desired. If the sort has several components, various levels of summation can become necessary. This is illustrated by the example shown in Fig. 3.8. This example is a project report with four levels of summation. The list is sorted by project, within project by product, within

PROJECT REPORT

PROJECT	PRODUCT	PERS.-NO.	NAME	TW	HOURS		
5050	QMS50	4711	MUSTERMANN, G.	PR	8.0		
5050	QMS50	4711	MUSTERMANN, G.	PR	8.0		
						*	16.0
5050	QMS50	4711	MUSTERMANN, G.	DO	8.0		
5050	QMS50	4711	MUSTERMANN, G.	DO	8.0		
						*	16.0
						**	32.0
5050	QMS50	1212	SCHMIDT, H.	PR	9.0		
5050	QMS50	1212	SCHMIDT, H.	PR	4.0		
						*	13.0
5050	QMS50	1212	SCHMIDT, H.	DO	5.0		
5050	QMS50	1212	SCHMIDT, H.	DO	7.0		
						*	12.0
						**	25.0
						***	57.0
5050	QMS75	4711	MUSTERMANN, G.	PR	8,0		
5050	QMS75	4711	MUSTERMANN, G.	PR	8,0		
						*	16.0
						**	16.0
						***	16.0
						****	73.0

Figure 3.8: Example of a sorted list with totals

product by personnel number and within personnel number by type of
work. Every time a break occurs in one of the sort fields a sum of the hours
is printed. The addition of the sums on any level of summation yields a
sum on the next higher level. The level of summation is indicated by one
or more asterisks. The lowest level of summation (i.e. the level on which
the sort control field changes most rapidly) has one asterisk; each higher

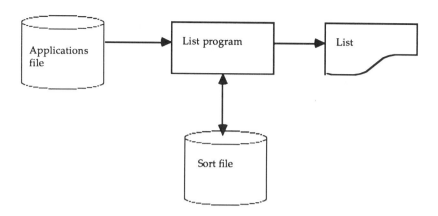

Figure 3.9: Systems flow chart for sorted
list with totals

level of summation has an additional asterisk. It is not unusual to have up
to six levels of summation in sorted reports of this type. Fig. 3.9 shows a
system flow chart, Table 3.3 a pseudocode logic for this type of application.

3.2.9 Transformation Program: One File => One File

In this type of application one file is copied into another and transformed
in some way during the process. The transformations can involve various
kinds of changes:

1. Reformatting.   The records in the output file have a different
format from those in the input file.

2. Computation.   Certain fields in the output file are derived by
arithmetic manipulation of fields in the input file.

3. Sorting.   The records in the output file are in a sequence
different from that of the input file.

Table 3.3: Pseudocode logic for sorted list with totals

```
OPEN FILES
IF SELECTION
   READ INPUT FILE UNTIL SELECTED RECORD
ELSE
   READ INPUT FILE
END-IF
UNTIL END OF FILE IN INPUT
   WRITE SORT WORK FILE
  IF SELECTION
     READ INPUT FILE UNTIL SELECTED RECORD
   ELSE
      READ INPUT FILE
   END-IF
END-UNTIL
UNTIL END OF FILE IN SORT WORK FILE
   READ SORT WORK FILE
   IF PAGE FULL OR FIRST TIME THRU
      PRINT HEADER LINES
   END-IF
   IF LOWEST ORDER CONTROL BREAK
      PRINT TOTAL LINE FOR LOWEST ORDER CONTROL BREAK
     RESET TOTAL COUNTER
     UPDATE COMPARISON FIELD
   END-IF
   IF NEXT HIGHER ORDER CONTROL BREAK
      PRINT TOTAL LINE FOR NEXT HIGHER ORDER CONTROL BREAK
     RESET TOTAL COUNTER
     UPDATE COMPARISON FIELD
   END-IF
         .
         .
         .
      ETC.
         .
   PRINT DETAIL LINE
   UPDATE TOTALS
END-UNTIL
CLOSE FILES
END
```

4. Selection.   The output file contains only a subset of the records
                       of the input file.

5. Summarization.   The record layout of the input file has a key and one
                       or more numeric fields. For each key there are
                       multiple records that have to be summarized into

one record. That means that the numeric values of all records with the same key are added up and output as one record. In order to accomplish this efficiently it is necessary that the input records be sorted in the sequence of the key in question.

6. Explosion.   Each record in the input file results in the generation of multiple records in the output file.

7. Supplementation.   The information in the input file is supplemented by additional information usually retrieved from tables.

An example of this type of processing is the following problem. A file for customer invoicing is to be created from a file containing time sheet data. Each employee of the company records his or her work time on a time sheet. Each segment of time is recorded keeping track of the customer for whom the work was done, the project code, the product code and the type of work. If an employee has not worked for a customer, the field for the customer code is left empty. Each line on the time sheet is recorded as a separate record in a file. The program reads the file with the time sheet data, selects those records with a customer code not equal to spaces, sorts the selected records in the sequence customer code/project code/product code/type of work/personnel number, summarizes the records (one per composite key) and outputs them in a different format to a file. An explosion technique would be necessary if, instead of one output record, several were required such as would be the case if debit and credit entries had to be generated. Fig. 3.10 shows a systems flow chart, Table 3.4 pseudocode logic for this type of application.

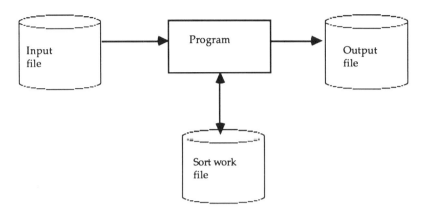

Figure 3.10: Systems flow chart for transformation program,
one file => one file

3.2.10 Transformation Program: One File => Multiple Files

This process is very similar to the previous case with the exception that instead of one output file, there are several. That would be necessary, for example, if a transaction file had to be split into several transaction files in order to provide several different systems with update data. The example given above can be extended to illustrate this type of model program. Assume that each customer needed a copy of its section of the time sheet data file. That would require that a separate file for each copy would have to be created. Fig. 3.11 shows a systems flow chart, Table 3.5 a pseudocode logic for this type of process.

3.2.11 Transformation Program: Multiple Files => One File

In this case one output file is created from multiple input files. There are two common variations on this theme:

1. Editing input data.   Each record of a transaction file is checked for
                          adherence to a set of validation rules; valid records

Table 3.4: Pseudocode logic for transformation program,
one file = > one file

```
OPEN FILES
UNTIL END OF FILE IN INPUT FILE
   IF SELECTION
      READ INPUT FILE UNTIL SELECTED RECORD
   ELSE
      READ INPUT FILE
   END-IF
   IF SUMMARIZATION
      READ INPUT FILE UNTIL CONTROL BREAK SUMMARIZING FIELDS
   END-IF
   IF SORT
      UNTIL END OF FILE IN INPUT FILE
         WRITE SORT WORK FILE
         IF SELECTION
            READ INPUT FILE UNTIL SELECTED RECORD
         ELSE
            READ INPUT FILE
         END-IF
         IF SUMMARIZATION
            READ FILE UNTIL CONTROL BREAK SUMMARIZING FIELDS
         END-IF
      END-UNTIL
      UNTIL END OF FILE IN SORT WORK FILE
         READ SORT WORK FILE
         FORMAT AND WRITE OUTPUT RECORD
         IF END OF FILE IN SORT WORK FILE
            SET PROGRAM END FLAG
         END-IF
   ELSE
      FORMAT AND WRITE OUTPUT RECORD
      IF END OF FILE IN INPUT FILE
         SET PROGRAM END FLAG
      END-IF
END-UNTIL
CLOSE FILES
END
```

---

are output to a file. One or more table files are used to validate the transaction records and/or to supplement the input data.

2. Master file update.   A master file is updated using a transaction file. The old version of the master file and the

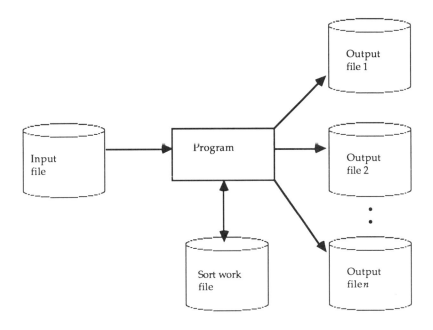

Figure 3.11: Systems flow chart for transformation program,
one file => multiple files

transaction file are the inputs, the new version of
the master file, the output.

In both cases there is one main file which controls the processing
logic. The transformations described in the previous examples such as
reformatting, sorting, selection, summarization, explosion and
supplementation may be necessary in the processing of the main file. In
practice, however, one would probably have the more complex
transformations such as sorting and explosion in a previous procedure in
order to have a better overview of the processing. Let us assume that the
time sheet data file from the example of the first transformation program
will be used as a transaction file to update a project master file. The
customer codes, project codes, product codes and types of work would first
have to be validated against tables of valid entries and the hours would
have to be converted into money amounts using a table of hourly rates.

Table 3.5: Pseudocode logic for transformation program
one file = > multiple files

```
OPEN FILES
UNTIL END OF FILE IN INPUT FILE
   IF SELECTION
      READ INPUT FILE UNTIL SELECTED RECORD
   ELSE
      READ INPUT FILE
   END-IF
   IF SUMMARIZATION
      READ INPUT FILE UNTIL CONTROL BREAK SUMMARIZING FIELDS
   END-IF
   IF SORT
      UNTIL END OF FILE IN INPUT FILE
         WRITE SORT WORK FILE
         IF SELECTION
            READ INPUT FILE UNTIL SELECTED RECORD
         ELSE
            READ INPUT FILE
         END-IF
         IF SUMMARIZATION
            READ FILE UNTIL CONTROL BREAK SUMMARIZING FIELDS
         END-IF
      END-UNTIL
      UNTIL END OF FILE IN SORT WORK FILE
         READ SORT WORK FILE
         FORMAT AND WRITE RECORD IN OUTPUT FILE-1
         FORMAT AND WRITE RECORD IN OUTPUT FILE-2
                •
                •
         FORMAT AND WRITE RECORD IN OUTPUT FILE-N
         IF END OF FILE IN SORT WORK FILE
            SET PROGRAM END FLAG
         END-IF
      END-UNTIL
   ELSE
      FORMAT AND WRITE RECORD IN OUTPUT FILE-1
      FORMAT AND WRITE RECORD IN OUTPUT FILE-2
                •
                •
      FORMAT AND WRITE RECORD IN OUTPUT FILE-N
      IF END OF FILE IN INPUT FILE
         SET PROGRAM END FLAG
      END-IF
END-UNTIL
CLOSE FILES
END
```

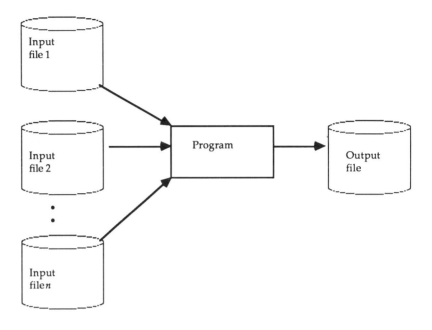

Figure 3.12: Systems flow chart for transformation program
multiple files = > one file

After that the project master file could be updated. Fig. 3.12 shows a systems flow chart, Table 3.6 pseudocode logic for this type of application.

3.2.12 Transformation Program: Multiple Files => Multiple Files

This model combines the characteristics of the transformation programs previously described. It is used for validation processes where transaction files have to be generated for several processes downstream and for update processes where several master files are maintained simultaneously. That might be the case, for example, if in the example cited above not just a project master file but also a customer master file had to be updated. Fig. 3.13 shows a systems flow chart, Table 3.7 pseudocode logic for such a process.

Table 3.6: Pseudocode logic for transformation program,
multiple files => one file

```
OPEN FILES
READ 1ST INPUT FILE
IF SUMMARIZATION
   READ 1ST INPUT FILE UNTIL CONTROL BREAK SUMMARIZING FIELDS
END-IF
UNTIL END OF FILE IN 1ST INPUT FILE
    READ CORRESPONDING RECORD IN 2ND INPUT FILE
    READ CORRESPONDING RECORD IN 3RD INPUT FILE
      •

      •
    READ CORRESPONDING RECORD IN NTH INPUT FILE
    FORMAT AND WRITE  RECORD IN OUTPUT FILE
    READ 1ST INPUT FILE
    IF SUMMARIZATION
       READ 1ST INPUT FILE UNTIL CONTROL BREAK SUMMARIZING FIELDS
    END-IF
END-UNTIL
CLOSE FILES
END
```

3.2.13 Menu Program

The last basic model program to be discussed is used to provide a easy way
to call up the programs of a software system. A menu program displays a
list of programs or suites of programs on a terminal screen. The user can
then select one of the possibilities. The menu program then either calls up
the selected program or, in the case of suites of programs, displays another
list. If a list is displayed, then the user must make a new selection. This
process is repeated until a list of application programs appears with which
the final selection of the desired program can be made. Systems consisting
of many hierarchically arranged subsystems have a hierarchy of selection
menus. Fig. 3.14 illustrates a typical menu hierarchy.

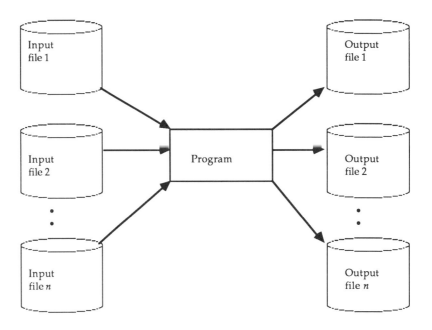

Figure 3.13: Systems flow chart for transformation program,
multiple files = > multiple files

3.3 The Interaction of the Basic Program Types

3.3.1 Centralized Table Maintenance

It is possible to solve any kind of commercial data processing problem using the three categories of files and the twelve basic model programs described above. Although the required system might involve hundreds of programs and files, it will, nevertheless, almost always be reducible to the interaction of a few basic types of models. In order to achieve an efficient interaction of the basic system components it is advisable to have a centralized table system as illustrated in Fig. 3.15. The centralized table system represents the core of the application system because it maintains certain types of information which control the interaction of the system components:

Table 3.7: Pseudocode logic for transformation program
multiple files => multiple files

```
OPEN FILES
READ 1ST INPUT FILE
IF SUMMARIZATION
   READ 1ST INPUT FILE UNTIL CONTROL BREAK SUMMARIZING FIELDS
END-IF
UNTIL END OF FILE IN 1ST INPUT FILE
    READ CORRESPONDING RECORD IN 2ND INPUT FILE
    READ CORRESPONDING RECORD IN 3RD INPUT FILE
    •
    •
    •
    READ CORRESPONDING RECORD IN NTH INPUT FILE
    FORMAT AND WRITE RECORD IN OUTPUT FILE-1
    FORMAT AND WRITE RECORD IN OUTPUT FILE-2
    •
    •
    •
    FORMAT AND WRITE RECORD IN OUTPUT FILE-N
    READ 1ST INPUT FILE
    IF SUMMARIZATION
        READ 1ST INPUT FILE UNTIL CONTROL BREAK SUMMARIZING FIELDS
    END-IF
END-UNTIL
CLOSE FILES
END
```

---

1. Validation tables.

These tables support the functions of checking and/or supplementing information contained in the application files of the system.

2. Parameter tables.

These tables contain information which determine the way certain programs perform their tasks. Exactly how this happens depends on the specific programs involved. Such tables lend more flexibility to the functionality of the programs by enabling variations in the programming logic without having to change the programs involved.

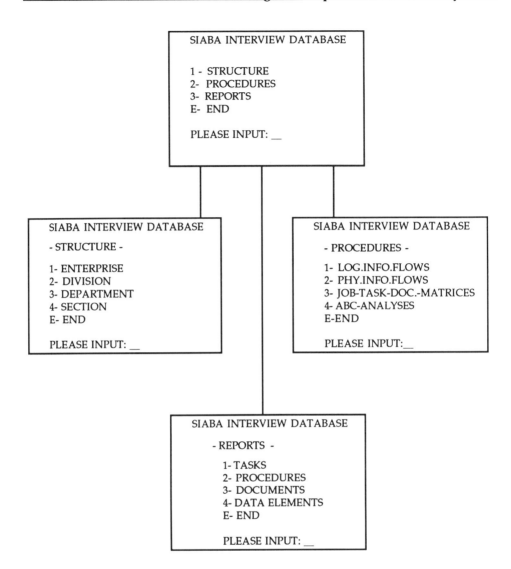

Figure 3.14: Example of a menu hierarchy

3. Access authorization tables.   These tables control user access to programs and tables. The contents of the tables determine what kinds of things a given user code is permitted to do.

4. Menu tables.

These tables store both the contents of selection menus as well as the menu hierarchy. Using this type of table makes it possible to have only a single menu program for an entire system. This one menu driver creates all selection menus and calls the individual programs selected. The menu driver can be organized in such a way that it takes the access authorization tables into consideration when creating the menus so that users only see functions that they are allowed to use.

5. Help information tables.

In the discussion of the database maintenance programs it was mentioned that each program should offer the option of displaying a description of how the program works. Such functional guidelines should be stored in tables so that they can be easily updated.

6. Message table.

All programs have occasion to display messages to the user (error messages, warnings, etc.). These kinds of messages should be standardized as much as possible and maintained in a central table.

These six kinds of tables define the basic rules for the interaction of the components of a software system. By maintaining this information in a centralized fashion it is easier to get an overview of the system and to maintain it more efficiently. Projects to extend the functionality of the system become more manageable. The advantages of this approach are very

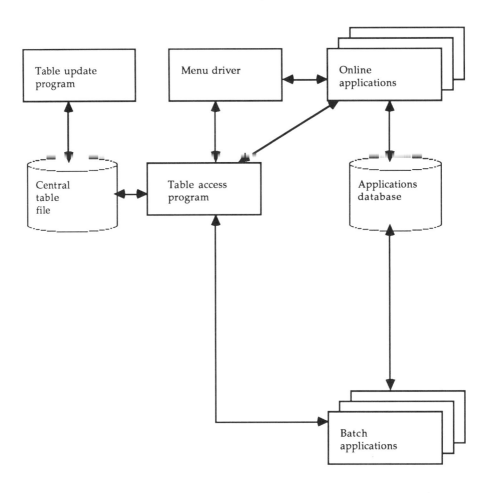

Figure 3.15: Centralized table management system

apparent if one considers the alternatives. A software system consisting of around 200 programs, for example, might have as many as 100 different kinds of tables. With the traditional approach without centralized table maintenance 100 additional programs would be required to maintain these tables. That means the lack of centralized table maintenance increases the number of programs required by 50 per cent. Unnecessarily high systems maintenance costs are the inevitable result. In addition, under these circumstances it would be unlikely that the programs would handle table access in a sufficiently integrated manner. With centralized table maintenance, however, table access always happens via one particular interface module that is used by all programs in a rigorously defined way.

3.3.2 The Activity File

The centralized table system contains applications systems information which changes relatively seldom. There are, however, other, more volatile types of information relating to the interaction of system components. It is not advisable to store this kind of information in the central table file because the effort to create new tables for such temporary information is not justifiable. In addition the relatively short key used in the central table file is often not adequate for the kinds of information being manipulated. Section 3.1.1 discussed briefly the function of the activity file - it functions as a type of work file for all programs of the system. As regards the interaction of application system components the main purpose of the activity file is the passing of messages between programs which are not active at the same time. Requests for batch processing are the most common example of this type of communication. In almost all systems there are processes that involve so many records that it would be highly inefficient to attempt to handle them in online mode. In such cases an online program stores a request for the batch process in the activity file. The request contains all parameters required for the execution of the batch process such as user ID, requested program and date and time of the request as well as all the variable control information that drives the batch process. This information is input using an interactive program corresponding to the first basic model program described earlier. That means the user can insert, alter, delete and view the request records. An example of this is illustrated in Fig. 3.16. In this example a request for the execution of a list program is being input which will create a project report from a project master file. The possible parameter variables include a time period and up to five project codes. This information is stored in the request record in the activity file. The requests are read later by a batch program called a starter

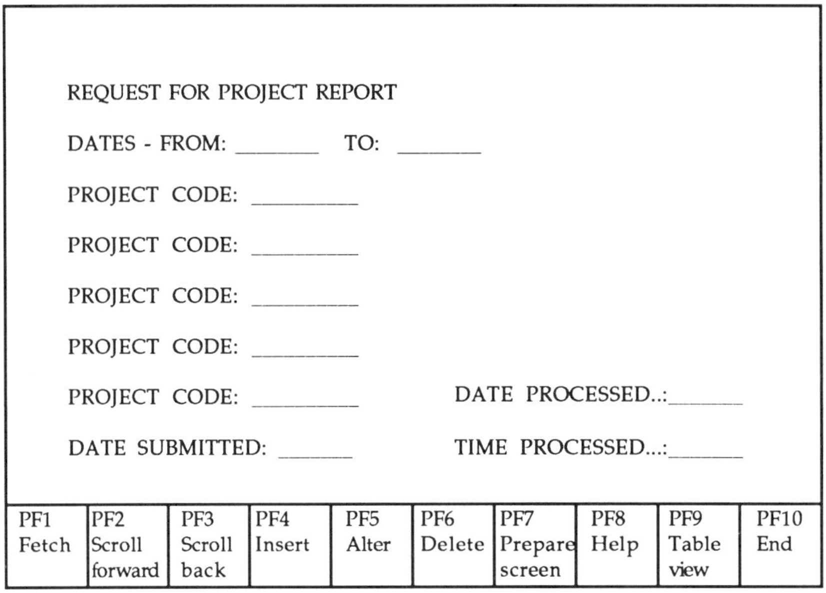

REQUEST FOR PROJECT REPORT

DATES - FROM: _____   TO: _____

PROJECT CODE: _____

PROJECT CODE: _____

PROJECT CODE: _____

PROJECT CODE: _____

PROJECT CODE: _____   DATE PROCESSED..:_____

DATE SUBMITTED: _____   TIME PROCESSED...:_____

PF1	PF2	PF3	PF4	PF5	PF6	PF7	PF8	PF9	PF10
Fetch	Scroll forward	Scroll back	Insert	Alter	Delete	Prepare screen	Help	Table view	End

Figure 3.16: Example of a screen layout for
maintaining batch processing requests

program. The starter program is initiated automatically at regular intervals by the operating system. The starter program scans the activity file for open requests and starts the desired processes. Each process at the conclusion of its work returns control to the starter program which then enters the date and time into the request record. The user who created the request can always examine the request record using the online program and determine whether or not the requested batch process has been completed. In this way batch processes can be entirely under the control of the users: the manual intervention of a job preparation clerk is no longer necessary. Direct user control of all processing becomes possible while at the same time avoiding excessive burdening of the system's teleprocessing monitor.

The central table file and the activity file are the core of a well-organized software system. Working together they enable the interaction of any number of programs in an unified and integrated fashion. The relationships among the systems components are illustrated in Fig. 3.17.

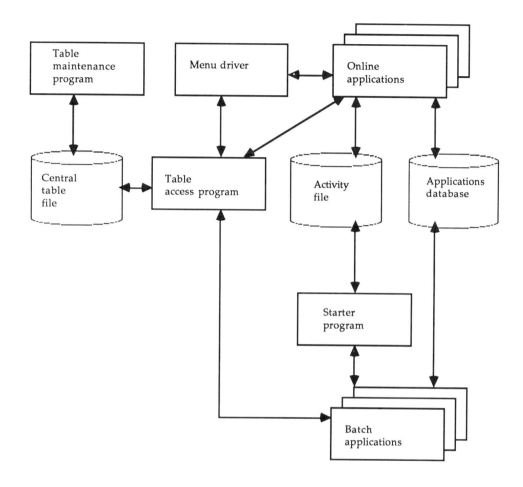

Figure 3.17: Interaction of the system components

This paradigm can be used for the construction of any commercial data processing system.

3.4 Review Questions and Exercises

1. List the three categories of files in an applications system.

2. What is the purpose of the activity file?

3. What kinds of information are stored in the table file?

4. What are the three categories of program in an applications system?

5. List the most important functions of a database maintenance program.

6. Discuss the most important kinds of processing that transformation programs accomplish.

7. What is a starter program?

8. What are some of the advantages of using standardized program modules?

4 From Documents to User Interface

After completion of the study of the current system as described in the second chapter, the SIABA database contains all the information necessary for defining a prototype. This collection of information implies many things about the organization, however, which are not always obvious at first glance. For this reason the information must be analyzed further in order to uncover the essential factors required for the design of the new system. In this chapter the further analysis of the current system will be discussed along with techniques for defining alternative systems' designs and evaluating those designs on the basis of cost/benefit analyses.

4.1 Analysis of the Current System

4.1.1 The Network of Logical Information Flows

In the second chapter the criteria for selection of the critical documents were described. The critical documents are those involved in tasks having a significant potential for improvement and those used by many people in the organization. These documents are the basis for the development of the user interface and must, therefore, be analyzed more precisely. The second chaper also described how the critical documents can be identified through the use of the ABC analyses. The documents indicated as critical by the ABC analyses are, however, not the only important documents. Each of these documents originates in some way that can be expressed by logical information flows. A logical information flow diagram shows the source documents from which a particular document is derived. These source documents can themselves have source documents, which in turn are derived from still other documents. In this way a logical information flow can involve a long series of documents with many interrelationships. The logical information flows of an organization can, therefore, take the form of a rather complex network. Fig. 4.1 shows a simplified example of such a network. If a document turns out to be critical, then all logical predecessor documents are also important. For example, if the list of open accounts in Fig. 4.1 is a critical document, then all documents to the left of it are important because the information contained in them is necessary for generating that list. The network of logical information flows plays an essential role in the design of any information system. This network determines what data must be captured and what transformations of these data are necessary to meet the information needs of the organization.

4.1.2 The Primary Documents

In order to develop strategies for the capture and transformation of data it is useful to divide the network of logical information flows into its component paths. Each path runs from a given document back over the source documents to one of the logical predecessor documents. The list of open accounts in Fig. 4.1, for example, has four paths:

1. List of open accounts => Accounts receivable => Invoice => Order.

2. List of open accounts => Accounts receivable => Bank statement.

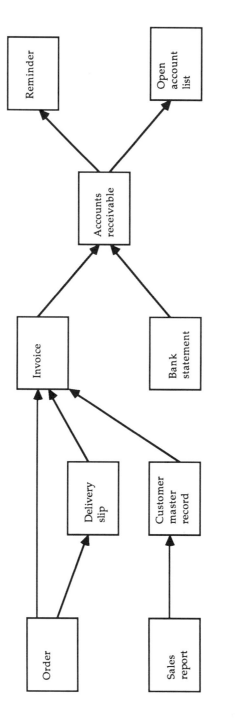

Figure 4.1: Example of a network of logical information flows

3. List of open accounts => Accounts receivable => Invoice => Delivery slip
    => Order.

4. List of open accounts => Accounts receivable => Invoice => Customer
    master record => Sales report.

At the beginning of each path is always a so-called primary document, i.e. a document which does not have source documents. Each logical information flow has its origin in one or more primary documents. If the organization is viewed as an information system, the primary documents are exogenous inputs into that system. In order to achieve the most efficient use of information, it is usually advisable to capture the data as soon as possible after their entry into the system. That means capturing the data from the primary documents and effecting the necessary transformations with the help of the computer. This results in a number of benefits:

1. The necessary transformations can be achieved with less human effort.

2. Useful transformations (for the most part mathematical and statistical analyses) can be performed which would either be impossible manually or only possible with an inordinate amount of time and effort.

The analysis of the logical predecessors of the critical documents illustrated in Table 4.1 provides a good overview of the typical kinds of transformations involved in the flow of business information. The paths described above from the critical documents to the primary documents are presented here in the form of a list. The critical documents are shown together with the codes of the work groups (WG) that use those documents. The logical predecessor documents are listed with the codes of the work groups where they originate. This list can be generated automatically from the SIABA database using the logical information flow file and the physical information flow file. This kind of analysis is a very useful guide for the systems designer´s investigations. One sees at a glance

Table 4.1: Analysis of the logical predecessors
of the critical documents

---Critical documents-----------			--------------Predecessor documents-----------			
		User				Originating
Doc. no.	Description	WG	Path	Doc. no.	Description	WG
4711	Open accts.	1005	1	4712	Accounts receiv.	1212
		1212		6001	Invoice	1212
				5454	Order	1003
			2	4712	Accounts receiv.	1212
				6001	Invoice	1212
				6003	Delivery slip	1004
				5454	Order	1003

the critical documents, where they are used, where they originate and from
what source documents they are derived. This list together with the
corresponding job-task-document matrices and the lists of tasks and work
steps per task provide a succinct overview of the current state of the
information system of an organization or subunit of an organization.

4.1.3 The Extended Data Element Analysis

In the course of the analysis of the current system the critical documents
were decomposed into their data elements. This analysis must now be
extended to the predecessor documents with the help of the list shown in
Table 4.1. The data elements of each document in each path must be
ascertained and recorded. Every data element is either taken over from a
predecessor document or generated through some transformation of other
data elements. The rules for such transformations must be recorded in the
data element rule file if that has not already been done as part of the
analysis of the current system. After completion of this task it must be

possible to determine the provenance of every data element in each critical document all the way back to the data elements of the primary documents. Only then does the systems designer have an overview of the information relationships of the current system sufficient for developing suggestions for new systems.

4.1.4 The Extended Job Analysis

The extended data element analysis may uncover gaps in the information about the job analyses performed in connection with the first part of the study of the current system. In the process of researching the origins of data elements one can run into documents and work groups that were not included in the original analysis. These must then be added. Job-task-document matrices for each missing work group must be created and the tasks of each of these work groups must then be broken down into their component work steps. It is important to make this extra effort because it is often the case that these 'up-stream' work groups play a more essential role in the data capture and transformation strategies of the new system than do the work groups originally analyzed.

4.2 Development of the New System Concept

4.2.1 Using the SIABA Database

With the help of the data stored in the SIABA database a new system concept can be built up in a step-by-step fashion. The raw material for this endeavour is a copy of the database. The data in the SIABA database represent a model of the way the organization operates in its current state. The new system can be described using exactly the same model. Much of the information in the new system will, of course, be processed and presented in a different way (e.g. in the form of screens or printouts); the new media will, however, relate to human tasks in some way just as their manually created counterparts in the old system did. In order to guarantee the success, acceptance and relevance of the new system it is essential to understand in detail the relationships between tasks and the information required to perform them. These relationships should, therefore, be taken into account already when designing screens and printouts. That means allocating the new screens and printouts to the tasks they are supposed to support. This is not to say that the tasks will not change in the new system. On the contrary, old tasks may be eliminated or simplified; new tasks will need to be defined. Job-task-document matrices and lists of the work steps per task should, however, be created for the new system in exactly the same way as for the old system. This forces the system designer to develop the necessary business procedures along with the other components of the system.

By copying and altering the SIABA database the system designer has the possibility of manipulating the model in many different ways until an acceptable concept for a new system emerges. In fact, multiple copies can be made in order to experiment with various alternatives. (It is important, however, to make a back-up copy of the original version of the database so that the state of the current system before all changes is properly documented.) Each copy of the SIABA database defines a possible information processing strategy for the organization and shows clearly what the consequences of implementing that strategy would be. In the first chapter it was pointed out that the failure of most computerization projects has to do with discrepancies between the functionality of the software used and the corresponding business requirements. By planning systems using a comprehensive enterprise model this problem can be avoided.

4.2.2 The Two Ways to Increase Organizational Efficiency

In designing a new system the main goals are the reduction of the effort needed for clerical work and the improvement of planning and control. Strategies for the reduction of the effort needed for clerical work are normally relatively simple to develop since they usually involve easily identifiable improvements in existing procedures. In practice, however, this type of efficiency gain is for the most part not nearly so financially significant as are improvements in planning and control mechanisms. For this reason it is prudent to concentrate primarily on strategies for increasing the efficiency of planning and control when developing a new systems concept.

Improving the efficiency of planning and control represents the more complex task because very often the information required does not yet exist in the organization (although it might be implicit in existing information). The critical documents are simply not there and must first be designed. After that has been accomplished, it is necessary to search for their logical predecessor documents. Again it is possible that this information is nowhere to be found in the organization. The systems designer might, therefore, have to develop whole new information flows, which might in turn involve very significant adjustments to the way the organization works. In the real world, however, most of the information required is normally available in some form somewhere in the organization. The systems designer then needs only to consider how the information can be transformed into a format appropriate for supporting the necessary decision-making processes and to integrate the new information flows into the existing networks of physical and logical information flows.

4.2.3 The Analysis of Problems and Goals

In developing strategies for the improvement of planning and control, one starts with the problems and objectives identified during the study of the current system and derives from them the information needs of the decision makers. In this process the system designer should not rely too heavily on the explicit wishes of the managers involved because they are very often unable to articulate their information needs in a comprehensive and optimal way. Managers frequently think they need a particular piece of information when in fact a different piece of information would actually be more useful. This is partly because many of them do not have an adequate knowledge of the possibilities of modern information technology and partly because most managers lack a sufficient overview of the information resources of the entire enterprise. It is, therefore, advisable to concentrate instead on the decision-making processes required for the attainment of goals and the solution of problems. In order to be able to make competent decisions certain specific information is needed. It is incumbent upon the systems designer to find out what information is going to have the optimal impact on the decision-making process. The systems designer should never seek to provide a particular item of information without understanding its relationship to the decision-making process, just because some user has expressed the desire to have it. Much wasted effort in software projects can be traced to this error.

In order to identify the information needed for decision-making it is necessary to analyze the different types of decisions. Managers make three basic kinds of decisions: strategic, tactical and operational. The systems designer must look for information that is helpful in the following decision-making processes:[1]

1. Identifying opportunities for the company in the market-place (strategic decision-making).

2. Describing the long-range goals and strategies of the company (strategic decision-making).

3. Evaluating goals and strategies (strategic decision-making).

4. Developing marketing systems, manufacturing systems, financial and other systems within the company which are related to the total operational system of the company (operational decision-making).

5. Developing standards of performance, methods of measurement and methods of control over long-range and operational activities (tactical and operational decision-making).

6. Achieving greater effectiveness (reaching goals) and greater efficiency (decreasing costs) (tactical and operational decision-making).

7. Preventing disasters (strategic, tactical and operational decision-making).

The search for this information was already begun in the first part of the study of the current system and must now be continued and intensified. The systems designer has to find out part of the information required for decision support in order to make a first attempt at estimating potential benefits. The estimate presupposed a basic approach to improving efficiency which must now be defined more concretely, and elaborated and refined.

The process of concretization involves for the most part the designing of screens and lists, the contents of which will influence decision-making. In designing screens and lists the systems designer is forced to define concrete concepts on the level of specific data elements. The data stored in the SIABA database about the old system can be very helpful here. The decision processes of the managers are recorded as tasks and the information needed for these tasks as documents. Many of the data elements needed for the design of the new information media can be extracted from these documents.

The data elements of the old system by themselves, however, are not always sufficient for designing the new media. After all, many problems in decision-making result from deficiencies in the available information. In this case it is necessary to develop new data elements. There are three methods to determine such additional information requirements:

1. Surveying the managers by traditional means, e.g. with questionnaires or interviews.

2. Analyzing the decision processes with artificial intelligence techniques.

3. Utilizing standard models and techniques such as those of operations research.

Surveying the Managers

To determine the additional information requirements it is often necessary to survey the managers involved. An example of an appropriate questionnaire is illustrated in Table 4.2.[2] With this instrument a marketing manager is queried very specifically about his or her information needs. Unlike in the study of the current system we are looking here for new information which is not to be found in the organization in its current state. The systems designer uses the answers gleaned in this survey to make suggestions about the contents of screens and lists. Such suggested layouts should contain real data and be stored in a word processing system to allow easy revision. Each screen and list example should be accompanied by a short verbal description of its application. These examples can then be printed out and given to the manager involved with the question, 'If information were available in this form, would it solve your decision-making problem?' If the response is negative, then the suggestions must be revised.

Analyzing the Decision Processes with Artificial Intelligence

A problem that frequently arises in determining additional information requirements is insufficient knowledge about the decision process on the part of the system designer. In order to be able to design a meaningful questionnaire the systems designer must have an accurate overview of the parameters of the decision-making process. In theory the steps of the decision process are already stored as work steps in the work step file; in practice these often turn out to be not sufficiently precise. If the decision-making process is not understood in detail, it is hardly possible to define the information needed to support it. One way to get this kind of detailed knowledge is to analyze the decision process with artificial intelligence techniques. In recent years very reasonably priced easy-to-use expert system shells have become available on PCs. They can be a very useful tool for the systems designer. These systems maintain so-called knowledge bases which are files containing rules, decision factors and suggestions. A knowledge base is processed by an inference engine. An inference engine is a program which asks the user questions and makes suggestions on the basis of the

Table 4.2:   Example of a questionnaire for ascertaining
              information requirements

___

Position: Marketing Manager

1. What information would you like to have to help you estimate
    market potential and forecast sales?

2. Would you like information on structural change of our
    industry such as mergers, new competitors, etc., in addition to
    the information you are now getting?

3. What information would help you with pricing decisions?

4. What additional information about customers do you desire?

5. What additional information would help you to find, evaluate,
    and select new products for your company?

6. What additional information do you need to make product
    decisions on mix, lines of products, warranties, price/quality
    combinations, etc.?

7. What additional information do you need to control sales
    operations?

8. What type of information would help you in making major
    promotional decisions?

9. Are you obtaining adequate information on new technological
    developments? Government and legal actions?

10. Do you need more information on channels of distribution?
    Physical distribution?

___

answers to these questions. The better systems can include external sources
of information as supporting information in the question and answer

rounds. Such information might be texts, graphics or output from a spreadsheet program. The decision-making process of a manager can be modelled in this fashion. The suggestions are then the decisions that the manager would make under the given circumstances.

This software can be used deductively or inductively. In **deductive** mode an expert system is constructed by defining a logic table with rules, facts and suggestions. This procedure is appropriate when a real expert is available. The logic table gives the system designer a clear overview of the steps in the decision-making process. The facts and any external data sources provide tips about the information requirements of the new system. With the help of the logic table the data in the work step file, the data element file and the document file can be fine-tuned.

The **inductive** approach involves making generalizations from empirical examples. This method is appropriate if no expert is available or for some reason clarity cannot be obtained about the rules of the decision-making process. In this case the decision process is divided into factors that can have varying values and results which represent the possible decisions. Then a comprehensive collection of examples is recorded. On the basis of these examples the artificial intelligence software works out the logical rules automatically. This technique is particularly useful if it is desired to determine the logical rules implicit in a collection of historical data. After this is done the data in the work step file, the document file and the data element file should be adjusted accordingly.

Using Standard Models and Techniques
Another method for finding out what data elements are needed for the design of the new information media is the use of standard models and techniques such as those used in operations research. For almost every aspect of an enterprise there exists well-tested quantitative models which can be adopted in whole or in part. These include linear programming techniques, queuing theory, mathematical inventory models, etc. Tips for the application of these techniques are to be found in textbooks, professional publications and software handbooks. Such sources should be systematically perused if the systems designer is not aware of an

appropriate model for a particular decision problem. As in the case of the survey approach, the suggestions here should be drawn up in the form of screen and list layouts and discussed with the managers involved.

Storing the Results of the Analysis

In practice both the surveying of managers as well as the research of standard solution models are essential for the development of an optimal user interface for the facilitation of decision-making. Both methods must be applied alternately until the managers involved are convinced of the utility of the screens and lists being designed. After that has been accomplished the planned screens and lists are added to the SIABA database as new documents and marked as being critical. In the document file the field 'system name' is filled in with the name of the planned system. This field can be used later to group all the media of the computerized information system together and to distinguish them from the information media of the manual information system. As with the documents of the old system these screens and lists must be assigned to the relevant tasks or decision processes. It also might be necessary to make appropriate adjustments to the work steps involved with these tasks and decision processes. If, for example, a manual card file used for a particular task is replaced by an interactive terminal display, changes in the work steps associated with that task are inevitable. New work steps such as calling up a program will become necessary, others which can be performed by the computer will be eliminated. All these kinds of changes must be documented in the SIABA database so that the organizational consequences of the proposed system are clearly visible.

After the new information media have been designed and assigned to the tasks that require them, the data elements involved are stored in the data element file. These new screens and lists must also be integrated into the existing information flows. That means that source documents, source data elements and data element rules must be defined. If no sources can be identified within the organization, they will either have to be created anew or sought in external data sources (such as public databases or data services). In any case, primary documents must be established which provide the required information. The creation of such new information flows can involve the definition of new tasks or even new jobs. This information as well must be recorded in the job file, the task file and the work step file because it will have a significant impact upon the cost/benefit analyses. In this case the additional costs resulting from the new tasks must be stored as a negative savings potential in the task file.

Through this procedure the data collection of the study of the current system is supplemented by the lists and screens needed for the improvement of planning and control. Now data capture and transformation strategies can be developed that enable the efficient processing of the information in such a way as to minimize the clerical work involved.

4.2.4 The Design of Data Recording, Transformation and Display Strategies

After integration of the lists and screens needed for the improvement of planning and control into the network of information flows the data collection for the proposed system is complete. The data collection will exhibit at this point, however, an unacceptably high level of redundancy. That is because in every large organization there are many groups that operate more or less autonomously having relatively little communication with each other; each of these groups typically maintains separate manual systems to maintain the data they use. These groups often use and process the same data without being aware of it. That results in an unnecessary multiplication of the same or similar work processes which means, of course, wasted effort and data inconsistency. Through analysis and integration it is possible to reduce the sources of data and thereby achieve a greater economy of data processing. A side effect of this effort is increased savings through the reduction of clerical work.

The procedure for data analysis and integration is best illustrated by a matrix of information outputs and the corresponding information sources. This matrix is an alternative representation of the logical information flows and can easily be generated automatically using the data stored in the

SIABA database. Fig. 4.2 show two matrices of information sources and outputs, one before the analysis and one after. By examining the information sources and outputs as well as the associated data elements and transformation rules the systems designer will discover many redundancies and can eliminate them. Some data sources will no longer be needed; others will be used by a wider group of people. After completion of this process information resources will be much more highly integrated and can, therefore, be used more thoroughly and efficiently.

In the light of the knowledge gained in the process of integration the analysis of the logical predecessors of the critical documents shown in Table 4.1 should be examined once again. This time, however, the analysis is generated from the version of the SIABA database which contains the data for the planned system. On the basis of this analysis of predecessor documents appropriate data collection strategies can be developed with the emphasis on primary documents. It is normally desirable to strive to capture the data of the primary documents in those work groups in which the documents originate or cross the systems' boundary of the organization for the first time. For this purpose, database maintenance programs must be designed which fit well into the existing procedures of the work groups in question. The first five basic model programs described in the third chapter are the building blocks for this task.

Once the data elements of the primary documents have been captured, all subsequent documents can be derived by transformation of the appropriate primary data elements. These transformations involve reformatting, calculation, sorting, selection, summarization, explosion or supplementation. The data element rule file provides the basis for defining these transformations. The systems designer must develop processes that accomplish these transformations in a reliable, auditable fashion with a minimum of human intervention. The four basic transformation programs described in the third chapter serve as models for the design of these processes. The analysis of the logical predecessors of the critical documents is very helpful here; the critical documents are the final goals of the transformations, the paths from the primary documents to the critical documents show the development stages. By the use of appropriate

Before the analysis

Information sources \ Information outputs	NPV analysis	Requirements analysis	Inventory file	Inventory list	Accounts receivable	Schedule	Shipping papers	Picking list	Customer master file	Delivery slip	Reminder	VAT report	Open order list	Open account list	Invoice	Turnover report	Sales statistics	Reservation
List of deductions												•						
Order									•						•			
Inventory card					•													
Accounts payable											•			•				
Schedule							•											
Bank statement					•													
Chart of accounts	•																	
Customer master record														•				
Inventory report			•															
Stock slip													•					
Stock list				•														
Delivery order									•									
Delivery slip																	•	
Invoice					•													
Reservation																		•
Turnover report		•																
Sales statistics														•				
Sales rep report																•		
Sales report									•									

After the analysis

Information sources \ Information outputs	NPV analysis	Requirements anal.	Inventory file	Inventory list	Accounts receiv.	Schedule	Shipping papers	Picking list	Customer master	Delivery slip	Reminder	VAT report	Open order list	Open account list	Invoice	Turnover report	Sales statistics	Reservation
Order		•	•	•		•		•		•			•		•		•	•
Accounts receivable	•	•								•				•				
Bank statement	•				•													
Customer master record						•	•								•			
Delivery slip			•	•			•						•		•		•	
Invoice	•				•						•			•		•		
Sales report								•										

Figure 4.2: Matrix of information sources and outputs

transformation programs the number of development stages can usually be reduced, resulting in increased efficiency.

Some transformations can be accomplished interactively as part of the data recording processes. This is feasible for transformations involving a relatively small number of records. Other transformations require the processing of large amounts of data and are, therefore, handled more efficiently in batch. In an inventory control system, for example, the updating of the inventory levels in the stock master file can easily be done as part of the process for recording issues and receipts. The creation of a suggested order list on the other hand necessitates scanning the entire stock master file and should, therefore, be handled as a batch process.

The system designer must investigate the various transformations required and decide which ones should be done interactively and which in batch. The factors that must be taken into consideration for this decision are the following:

1. The amount of data to be processed.

2. The operational characteristics of the teleprocessing monitor and the database management system.

3. The desired response times for the interactive processes (minimum requirement = less than three seconds).

In order to conceptualize the various processes needed for the new information system, the systems designer begins with the recording of the primary documents and works his/her way through the network of logical information flows to the critical documents. The intermediate documents encountered along the way are the nodes of the system where transformations occur and/or additional data are recorded. In order to be able to propose appropriate solutions for systems it is necessary to understand the task-document relationships at each node. During the analysis of the manual transformations it often turns out that some intermediate documents are only used to produce other documents and have no direct connection to essential tasks. An example of this might be an invoicing worksheet that is used for the manual preparation of invoices. If the invoices are to be automatically generated in a new computerized invoicing system, then the invoicing work sheet and all work processes associated with it can be eliminated because the required transformations will be completely taken over by the computer. In this case both the intermediate document and the node cease to exist, and manual effort will be reduced in the new information system. Other intermediate documents turn out to be essential for the performance of certain tasks and must, therefore, be retained. It may still, however, be possible to improve their format or produce them with less manual effort.

After the data capture and transformation strategies have been defined, information display strategies must be developed which are based on the critical documents. The information will normally be displayed in the form of a screen or printed list. For the screen displays, simpler versions of the database maintenance programs can be used. The storage functions are merely removed from the programs. The user can access, display and scroll the data from the database. The lists are created with programs corresponding to the two basic list programs described in the third chapter. The development of the display strategies is important and time consuming but not particularly difficult because at this stage of the project all the required data elements are known. The systems designer has only to compose layouts of the data elements associated with the critical documents in such a way that hardware constraints and work requirements are satisfied.

4.3 Cost/Benefit Analyses

4.3.1 Estimating the Development Costs

If the proposed system is defined in terms of a SIABA database, it becomes very easy to estimate the development costs. In the sections above it was explained how the information media of the new system are stored in the document file as lists and screen layouts. The user interface of the new system consists of precisely these lists and screen layouts which are identified in the file by a system name and a program name. (Manual documents have no information in these fields.) Since all model programs adhere to the principle 'one program = one list or one screen display', the document file provides a good overview of the program modules needed for the proposed system. The way the list or screen produced by a given module is to be used is apparent from the description of the associated task and the work steps connected with that task. The field, 'PROGRAM TYPE', contains the number of a particular model program. Since the model programs are based on reusable components, it is a simple matter to work out a standard cost rate for each model. If the standard cost rates are stored in a parameter table, the total costs for all system modules can easily be generated automatically.

In order to generate the module cost report automatically the systems designer must review all computerized screens and lists stored in the document file and fill in the fields 'SYSTEM NAME', 'PROGRAM NAME' and 'PROGRAM TYPE'. The system name field can be used to group the programs into different subsystems. The definition of subsystems is usually related to the subdivisions of the work groups in the organization. The program name field identifies the document as part of a software system. The specification of a program type enables the automated standard cost calculation. The inputting of this information during the maintenance of the document file causes the standard cost rate to be accessed automatically from a parameter file and stored in the appropriate document record. This value can be overridden by the systems designer if there is any reason to believe that the costs of the given module are going to be significantly different from the standard. In practice this should not be necessary very often if the standard costs have been calculated properly.

After completion of the standard cost calculation the SIABA database provides a good overview of the planned system. The module cost report shown in Table 4.3 can now be generated and defines the scope of the development project. The distribution of users is also defined by the task-document relationships stored in the SIABA database. On the basis of this

Table 4.3: Module cost report

Program module	Description	Planned costs	Actual costs
PPMS1000	Maint. Personnel Master	1,500	
PPMS2000	Maint. Project Master	1,800	
PPMS3000	Maint. Product Master	1,700	

information the work group/program matrix illustrated in Fig. 4.3 can be created automatically. Together, these two documents show how large the planned system is, how expensive the development of the modules will be and who will use these modules.

4.3.2 Estimating the Benefits

While the costs in SIABA are recorded in the document file, the quantifiable benefits are stored as potential savings in the task file. These potential savings were roughly estimated during the first part of the analysis of the current system. At this point in the project the systems designer should review these estimates for the percentage reduction of clerical work and the improvements of planning and control and adjust them in light of the more comprehensive collection of information now available. The estimates of potential benefits always play an essential role in project budget negotiations and are scrutinized very critically by top management. For this reason it is often advisable to subject the benefits estimates to a refinement round with the managers involved in order to develop a convincing consensus. The analysis of the benefits per work group shown in Table 4.4 is very helpful in such a process. This analysis together with the work group/program matrix illustrated in Fig. 4.3 provides a good basis for the discussions.

Work groups \ Programs	PPMS1000	PPMS2000	PPMS2200	PPMS2300	PPMS2400	CCMS1000	CCMS1500	CCMS2000	CCMS2700	CCMS3000	CCMS4000	CCMS5000	CCMS5500	STAT1000	STAT2000
Accounting	•	•				•									
Stock room			•											•	•
Manufacturing				•		•		•							
Sales										•	•			•	•
Design					•				•						
Personnel	•					•						•	•		

Figure 4.3: Work group/program matrix

4.3.3 Financial Analysis and Documentation of the New System Concept

Once the standard costs have been calculated and the benefits' estimates adjusted, the SIABA database provides the basis for further quantitative analyses. Since the alternative systems concepts are stored as separate SIABA databases, these analyses can be used to compare various solution approaches. The alternative with the most favourable quantitative characteristics is usually the one that should be implemented.

The most important quantitative dimension of the planned system is the net total benefit. The net total benefit is ascertained through a net present value analysis. In a net present value analysis the costs and benefits of a proposed system are calculated for the entire life of the system. Future cash flows are then discounted by the amount of the expected average interest rate so that present monetary values can be compared. (For example, a dollar that is going to be received a year from now is worth less than a dollar today because a dollar available today could be invested and earn a year´s worth of interest.) The variables in this process are the assumptions concerning the average interest rate and the length of the life of the system. The software development costs are usually allocated to the

Table 4.4: Benefits per work group

WG Code	Work group	Task	Planned benefits	Actual benefits
1000	Accounting	Invoicing	20,000	
1000	Accounting	Open account list	80,000	
1200	Sales	Direct mail camp.	50,000	
1200	Sales	Telephone sales	120,000	
1500	Stock room	Ordering	250,000	

first year of system usage, the expected maintenance costs proportionately to the remaining years of the system's life. The benefits are already stored in the task file in annualized form; they need only be extrapolated for the total years of system usage. In this way two cash flows are input, one for the costs and one for the benefits for each year of the system's expected life. To arrive at the net present value the values of these two series are discounted using the following formula:

$$\sum_{i=1}^{n} \frac{V_i}{(1+x)^i}$$

In this formula V stands for the individual values of each series, x is the interest rate and n the number of periods (in this case, years). These calculations can easily be automated. The screen shown in Fig. 4.4 can be used to input the parameters necessary for a process which performs the net present value analysis based on the data stored in the SIABA database. In addition to interest rate and length of the life of the system, the percentage of total costs that maintenance is expected to require is input (default = 70 per cent). It is also possible to input design expenditures if these are to be included in the calculation. On the basis of these parameters the program performs the net present value calculation and prints the report shown in Table 4.5. This analysis is simplified in that some factors such as inflation and changes in payroll costs are left out. It is sufficient for the practical purpose of comparing various alternatives, however, because

```
┌─────────────────────────────────────────────────────────────────────┐
│                                                                       │
│                                                                       │
│          CALCULATION OF NET PRESENT VALUE ANALYSIS                    │
│          WITH THE  FOLLOWING PARAMETERS:                              │
│                                                                       │
│          TIME PERIOD........................................:  __     │
│                                                                       │
│          INTEREST  RATE................................:  __          │
│                                                                       │
│          DESIGN COSTS..............................:  _____      │
│                                                                       │
│          MAINTENANCE COSTS AS % OF TOTAL COSTS.........:  ____        │
│                                                                       │
│                                                                       │
│                                                                       │
│                                                                       │
├──────┬──────┬──────┬──────┬──────┬──────┬───────┬─────┬──────┬────────┤
│ PF1  │ PF2  │ PF3  │ PF4  │ PF5  │ PF6  │ PF7   │ PF8 │ PF9  │ PF10   │
│ Fetch│Scroll│Scroll│Insert│Alter │Delete│Prepare│Help │Table │End     │
│      │forward│back │      │      │      │screen │     │view  │        │
└──────┴──────┴──────┴──────┴──────┴──────┴───────┴─────┴──────┴────────┘
```

Figure 4.4: Screen layout for net present value analysis

the factors left out affect all alternatives in more or less the same way. This report should be generated for each alternative. The best alternative is the one with the greatest positive net total benefit.

In addition to the net present value analysis a comparison of the marginal benefits and marginal costs of the system components can be very instructive (see section 1.2.1). The marginal benefit is the addition to the total benefits that the computerization of one more task provides. The marginal costs, on the other hand, are the costs incurred for the development of the software components necessary to achieve that benefit. This analysis helps to determine the optimal scope of the system. In Section 2.2.5 the ABC analysis of potential benefits was discussed. This analysis shows the improvable tasks in descending sequence of potential benefits. In the determination of the optimal scope of the system it is appropriate to be guided by the sequence of this list.

After the user interface has been defined, the tasks listed in the ABC analysis map to system components stored in the document file. Each task

Table 4.5: Net present value analysis

Interest rate: 8.0 %   Period: 10 years   Maintenance as %: 70.0%

Year	Costs	NPV	Benefits	NPV
1	750,000	694,444		
2	194,444	166,704	400,000	342,936
3	194,444	154,356	400,000	317,533
4	194,444	142,922	400,000	294,012
5	194,444	132,335	400,000	272,233
6	194,444	122,533	400,000	252,068
7	194,444	113,456	400,000	233,396
8	194,444	105,052	400,000	216,108
9	194,444	97,270	400,000	200,100
10	194,444	90,065	400,000	185,277
		---------------		--------------
Totals:		1,819,137		2,313,663
Net benefits:				494,526

has a potential benefit which corresponds to costs of particular system components. It is, therefore, possible to generate the comparison of marginal benefits and marginal costs illustrated in Fig. 4.5. These two curves show marginal costs and marginal benefits for different scopes of the system. Since this analysis is done in the sequence of the ABC analysis, the greatest benefits are on the left-hand side of the diagram. From there the marginal benefits curve sinks continuously illustrating the law of diminishing returns. The marginal cost curve, on the other hand, usually has the shape of a flattened U. It is reasonable to increase the scope of the system until the marginal costs equal the marginal benefits, i.e. until the two curves intersect. A system scope at any point to the left of the intersection means that there are neglected opportunities for computer-ization where the marginal benefits exceed the marginal costs. A system

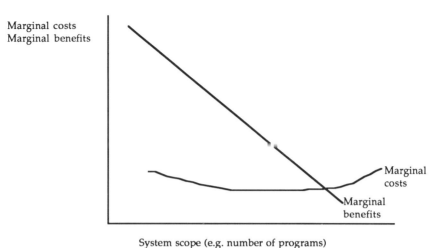

Marginal costs
Marginal benefits

Marginal
costs

Marginal
benefits

System scope (e.g. number of programs)

Figure 4.5: Comparison of marginal costs and marginal benefits

scope at any point to the right of the intersection indicates that some computerization steps are not worth their costs. It is advisable, therefore, to generate these curves for each alternative system proposal and use them to determine the optimal scope of the system.

After the scope of the system has been determined, it is appropriate to examine the distribution of costs and benefits among the various work groups. The cost/benefit report per work group shown in Table 4.6 is used for this purpose. In this analysis the costs and benefits calculated in the net present value analysis are distributed to the different work groups involved. Since the costs in the SIABA model are allocated to the documents, however, there is no direct way to allocate them to the work groups. Moreover, the same documents are often used by many different work groups. For these reasons the costs are first allocated proportionately to the work groups on the basis of the task-document relationships. To simplify matters, each work group that uses a given document receives an equal cost allocation. If, for example, five work groups all use a particular document, each of them receives a cost allocation of one-fifth. The cost/benefit analysis per work group gives an overview of the distribution

Table 4.6: Cost/benefit analysis per work group

WG Code	Work group	Proportion of costs NPV	Proportion of benefits NPV
1000	Accounting	50,000	100,000
1200	Sales	150,000	170,000
1500	Stock room	100,000	250,000
Totals:		300,000	520,000

of computerization opportunities in the organization, thus aiding the definition of priorities for the rest of the project. The analysis can also be used to achieve a fair distribution of the development costs to the various cost centres.

The analyses described may uncover aspects of the proposed system(s) that need to be improved. These must then be revised appropriately. After that has been accomplished, each alternative proposal should be documented by printing the reports shown in Table 4.7 from each of the SIABA databases. Each group of reports represents a possible system solution. The decision about which alternative to select can then be made on the basis of these documents.

4.4 Review Questions and Exercises

1. What is a primary document?

2. In what kinds of decision processes can information play an essential role?

3. After analyzing the current system how are the additional information requirements determined?

Table 4.7: System proposal

- Job-task-document matrix
- List of the work steps per task
- List of the work step rules
- Physical information flows
- Logical information flows
- List of objectives and subobjectives
- List of problems and possible solutions
- ABC analysis of potential benefits
- ABC analysis of information flows
- List of critical documents
- List of documents with data elements
- List of data elements, source elements and rules
- Analysis of the logical predecessors of the critical documents
- Matrix of information sources and outputs
- Module cost report
- Work group/program matrix
- Benefits per work group
- Net present value analysis
- Analysis of marginal costs and marginal benefits
- Cost/benefit analysis per work group

---

4. List the most important steps in the development of a systems
    proposal.

5. What is the use of a net present value analysis?

6. How is the optimal scope of a system determined?

4.5 Notes

[1]R. G. Murdick and J. E. Ross, *Information Systems for Modern Management*, Englewood Cliffs, N.J.: Prentice Hall, 1975, p. 367.
[2]R. G. Murdick and J. E. Ross, *Information Systems for Modern Management*, Englewood Cliffs, N.J.: Prentice Hall, 1975, p. 368.

5 The Integration of Users' Views

After the alternative system proposals have been developed in the manner described in the fourth chapter, the one with the greatest payout is selected. The chosen alternative contains all the data elements that will be processed in the new information system. These data elements are, however, spread over all the screens and lists of the system. The screens and lists constitute the users' views of the data, but have the disadvantage that they exhibit an excessive degree of redundancy because the same data elements are often found in many different screens and lists. In order to create an efficient information system a data model must be developed which integrates all the different user views. In this data model, redundant data elements are to be eliminated unless there is some specific reason to make an exception (e.g. to speed up response times). The logical relationships of the data elements to each other determine the structure of the data model. Through the process of normalization, the data model is structured in such a way that inconsistencies and redundancies are eliminated, providing an optimal basis for future growth and adaptability. In this chapter the principles and advantages of centralized data administration and normalized data models are explained. In addition the recording of the logical data model in the SIABA database is discussed.

5.1 The Necessity of Centralized Data Administration

5.1.1 The Problem of Insular Solutions

The data of an organization originate in its various functional areas. In order to cope with the daily work load, each work group records data in a way conducive to the performance of its tasks. For this reason there is a natural tendency to organize data according to functional principles. In the early years of data processing this resulted in the development of software systems that reflected the functional division of labour. The work group payroll accounting, for example, used a payroll system, financial accounting, a general ledger system, etc. Each work group concerned itself primarily with its own data in a relatively isolated way. Communication with other work groups was usually limited to sharing printed reports or (in very progressive companies) copies of files on magnetic media such as tapes. This way of organizing of information systems is illustrated in Fig. 5.1.

The traditional organization of information systems turned out to be very inefficient for a number of reasons:

1. Time lags in the flow of information. Every transfer of interface data requires time. In complex organizations it can take months before new information reaches all the work groups that need it. In such cases important decisions often cannot be made on time because the necessary information arrives too late.

2. Costs of information processing. The transfer of interface data frequently involves significant effort. It is often necessary to perform fairly complex transformations on the information in order to get it in the format that a given work group needs.

3. Data inconsistency. Identical or similar data elements are often stored in different formats in different systems. This usually hinders communication and can even make it impossible. Important reports needed for strategic decision-making often cannot be generated automatically because the data in the different areas are in incompatible

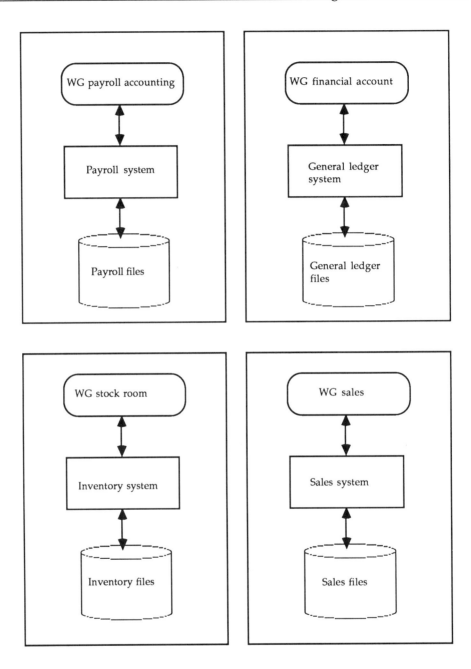

Figure 5.1: Traditional relationships among information systems

formats. Other reports only cause confusion because each area has its own version of a particular statistic and no one can understand why they are not the same.

In organizations characterized by growth and change these problems are like a time bomb. This becomes clear if the number of interfaces of an increasing number of systems is observed. If each of the four systems shown in Fig. 5.1 has two information flows to each of the other systems, there are a total of twelve information flows. If only one system is added, the number of information flows increases to twenty; with six systems there are already thirty flows. The growth of the number of interfaces can, therefore, become a geometric series. It becomes more and more expensive to maintain these information flows. Trivial changes in one system can have an immense (and often unforeseen) impact on the others. For these reasons it is generally accepted today that centralized data administration is to be preferred to insular system solutions.

5.1.2 The Advantages of a Centralized Data Model

A centralized data model is an essential component of any well integrated information system. In this model the data should not be organized according to functional area but rather according to the objects to which the data pertain. The reason for this is that the things about which data are stored are much less subject to change than are the functional procedures in which the data are used. In a typical middle-sized enterprise there are usually not more than a few hundred objects about which data are stored. New objects only appear when the business of the enterprise changes in a fundamental way. The business procedures, on the other hand, change continuously because the enterprise has to adapt to the daily challenges of its tasks and its environment. In order, therefore, to have a solid foundation upon which to build information systems, it is advisable to develop a centralized data model organized by data objects. An organizational scheme for this approach to information systems is illustrated in Fig. 5.2.

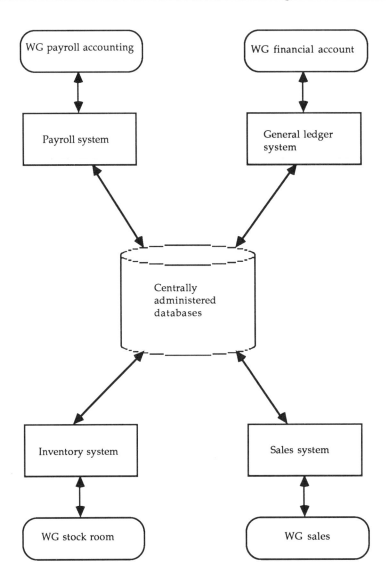

Figure 5.2: Information systems with centralized data administration

5.1.3 Entities, Attributes, Values and Extracts

The objects about which data are stored are often referred to as entities. Examples of entities in an industrial enterprise are invoices, warehouses, subsidiaries, employees, products, customers, orders, etc. Entities have particular attributes which are described by data elements. An invoice can have, for example, a customer address, item numbers, item descriptions, amounts, prices and totals. For a given instance of an invoice, each attribute has a specific value. While the values of the attributes can vary within certain limits, the entities themselves and their attributes remain relatively stable. There may, for example, be many thousands of different invoices in a given year, but each invoice has exactly the same basic structure. Since there are seldom more than a few hundred entities in an organization and each entity will have on average about ten attributes, it is appropriate to use entities and their attributes as the basic building blocks of the data model. In this way a data structure is obtained which, on the one hand, needs to be changed relatively seldom but, on the other hand, can be easily adapted to the natural growth of the organization. Many different data extracts can be developed from this kind of data structure. That is important because the changing nature of the typical business organization requires a continuous stream of new data extracts, most of which cannot be foreseen in the initial phases of a software development project. These needs can only be met effectively if the data structure is organized by entities and their attributes.

5.1.4 Identifying and Naming Data Elements

In the analysis up to now the names of documents and data elements were simply derived from whatever conventions happened to be in use in the organization under study. In the construction of a data model, however, it is necessary to apply a stricter set of rules. The home-grown conventions of the typical business organization are replete with redundancy and inconsistency. These weaknesses must be eliminated if an effective data administration is to be achieved. That means that comprehensive standards for the definition and naming of data elements must be established and adhered to.

Coupling and Cohesion
Data elements have two properties that play an essential role in the design of the data model: coupling and cohesion. A data element is said to be

coupled to another data element if the value of the first data element depends on the value of the second data element. In a group of data elements, for example, there is usually a key data element that determines the values of the other data elements, i.e. a logical coupling exists between the key and each of the other data elements. An important principle of data element definition is that such coupling should only exist between a given data element and the key; data element coupling among non-key data elements is to be eliminated. The process of normalization to be described later in this chapter is a method for minimizing data coupling.

In physics cohesion is the mutual attraction by which the elements of a body are held together, such as the molecules of a compound. In information science this word has an analogous meaning - it describes the force that holds a data element together. A data element can be seen as the elementary unit of an information system which cannot be subdivided further without losing its meaning. Many data elements which arise in business practice do not exhibit this quality. Take, for example, a data element in a customer information system which has the following name:

CUST-AREA-DISCOUNT

This data element consists of four characters: the first two indicate a geographic area while the second two specify a discount percentage. Such a data element is not cohesive because it really consists of two data elements:

CUST-AREA
CUST-DISCOUNT

When designing a data model such data elements must be split appropriately. In general, when defining data elements, it is advisable to maximize data element cohesion and minimize data element coupling in order to achieve a stable, flexible data model.

Data Element Naming Conventions
One important aspect of efficient data administration is the consistent use of data element naming conventions. Such conventions are essential in order to maintain an overview of the data model and to avoid redundancy.

Many studies have shown that the typical software system has about twenty times as many data element names as data elements.[1] This redundancy is a result of inadequate application of naming standards and can be significantly reduced by the establishment of and adherence to appropriate conventions.

The naming convention recommended in the SIABA approach provides for data element names consisting of a maximum of thirty characters. (That corresponds to the largest allowable field name in the Cobol programming language.) The name is made up of the following components:

1. A class designation.

2. A main component.

3. One or more additional components.

Class designations indicate something about the general purpose of the data element. Normally ten class designations are recommended:[2]

AMOUNT	NAME
CODE	NUMBER
CONSTANT	PERCENT
COUNT	TEXT
DATE	TIME

The main component is derived from the corresponding entity category or subcategory. INVOICE, CUSTOMER and ACCOUNTING are examples of entity categories. The additional components are used to ensure the uniqueness of data element names. The components of data element names are usually joined by hyphens. Some examples of data element names are:

INVOICE-NUMBER
CUSTOMER-NUMBER
PLAN-DATE-START

PLAN-DATE-END

Although it might seem odd to separate the components of the data element names by hyphens, this turns out to be very useful in many data dictionary systems. That is because such a convention makes it much easier to search for redundancies. The data elements of the data model can be sorted and listed by each of the components, allowing the data administrator to spot redundancies and inconsistencies quickly. Such sorted lists are also very useful when assigning new data element names.

The class designation, the main component and, if possible, the additional components should be standardized and documented for the entire organization. It is also advisable to establish a standard abbreviation for each designation. In addition, it is often possible to standardize the data definition of many class designations (e.g. DATE = two-digit year + three-digit day). The lists of name components are the guide for assigning the data element names of the centralized data model.

5.1.5 Data Independence and Database Management Systems

Another requirement for a stable data structure is the separation between the logical and physical aspects of information storage. The physical characteristics of information storage vary greatly among different types of storage units. Moreover, storage technology is one of the most innovative areas of electronic engineering. For these reasons a program will become obsolete very quickly if its functionality depends on the physical characteristics of a storage medium. In order to avoid the necessity of frequent adjustments it is, therefore, appropriate to insulate software as much as possible from the physical details of data storage. This is accomplished by having programs read and write their data in the form of logical views which are as independent of hardware as possible. This so-called data independence dramatically reduces the amount of maintenance effort necessary to support the growth of information resources in an enterprise.

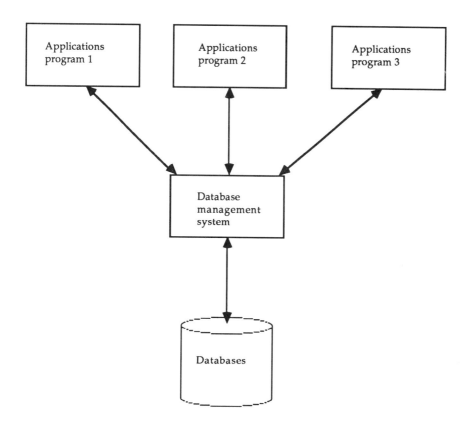

Figure 5.3: Database management system

One of the most common ways to strive for data independence is the use of a database management system (DBMS). A database management system mediates between programs and data structures (see Fig. 5.3). The programs communicate with the DBMS via data buffers which contain logical views of the data. The physical details of storage are handled by the DBMS. That means that the evolution of the data structure does not necessitate changes in existing programs as long as the corresponding logical views of the data do not change.

5.2 The Normalization of Data

Data normalization is a process for the logical grouping of data elements in order to maximize flexibility and minimize future problems. In normalized data groups (in the so-called third normal form) each data element maps into a particular key. The key can consist of one or more data elements. If a key consists of more than one data element, then the dependent data elements must depend on the whole key (not just on one part of the key). If the value of the key is determined, then the values of the rest of the data elements of the data group are also determined.

Keeping data structures in the third normal form has many advantages. The relationships among data elements adhere to simple, precise, logical rules. This makes utilization of the data much easier because simple data groups have fewer restrictions on the way they can be combined than more complex data groups. Extending the database to include new data elements is, therefore, less problematical. In addition, for a given data structure with defined dependencies among the data elements there is only one third normal form. For this reason the third normal form is a very useful standard for data organization since the results of a correctly performed normalization process are always the same, no matter who designs the database.

The process of normalization consists of three steps: a data group is first transformed into the first normal form, then into the second and finally into the third normal form. In the next sections these three steps will be explained with the help of an example.

5.2.1 The First Normal Form

In order to demonstrate the process of normalization the data elements of the invoice shown in Table 5.1 will be analyzed. This is an invoice used by an data processing consulting company to bill its customers. The main business of this consulting company is contract programming. The service consists of providing experienced programmers who create software systems for the client. Once a month the hours worked by the programmers are billed to the clients. Each detail line on an invoice

Table 5.1: Invoice of a data processing consulting company

Cust.No. 1542

XYZ Corp.
Post Box 4711
Eldred, New York 12732

27 Aug. 90

Invoice No. 89001

Billing Period	Personnel No.	Name	Program	Hrs.	Fee/Hr.	Total
Jan.89	1020	Schmidt	PSX4000	60	100	6,000.00
Jan.89	1030	Fischer	BMP2000	50	90	4,500.00
Jan.89	1040	Bach	PQT3000	70	90	6,300.00
						16,800.00
				+ 15% Tax		2,520.00
						19,320.00
						========

corresponds to the time spent for a particular programmer on a particular program in the given time period. Through the process of normalization the optimal data structure for storing the data elements of this invoice will be developed.

The first step involves the determination of the data elements which make up the invoice. In this process it is not necessary to consider data fields that can be calculated. Since these fields can be produced at any time with simple arithmetic manipulations, it is not necessary to store them in the database. The data elements which need to be stored in this case are illustrated in Fig. 5.4. The arrows show the logical relationships among the data elements. The main key is the invoice number which

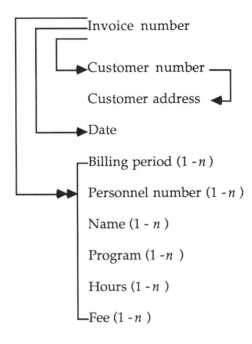

Figure 5.4: Data elements of an invoice

determines the customer number, the invoice date and the detail lines. The customer address depends on the customer number. The double arrow between the invoice number and the data elements of the detail line indicates a one-to-n relationship, i.e. an invoice can have multiple detail lines. The other relationships are one-to-one relationships; an invoice number can, for example, have only one customer number and one invoice date.

In order to store this unnormalized data group it is necessary to make an assumption about the maximum number of detail lines that could occur in an invoice. The systems designer has to find out what the largest number of detail lines is that could ever be necessary and define the record layout accordingly. If this assumption ever turns out to be incorrect, then the record layout must be revised and all programs using it must be altered. In addition, the record will always require a storage space big enough for the largest possible invoice, a fact which will almost certainly waste significant amounts of storage capacity. The one-to-n relationship can result, therefore, in inefficient usage of storage and maintenance problems in the future. For these reasons the transformation of data groups into the first normal form involves the removal of one-to-n relationships. This is done by splitting the data group. The data group shown in Fig. 5.4 is split into the two data groups illustrated in Fig. 5.5. If the invoice data are stored in this form, it is no longer necessary to make any assumptions about the maximum number of detail lines; each detail line will be stored as a separate record of which there can be any number.

5.2.2 The Second Normal Form

The determination of the second normal form has to do with the functional dependencies among the data elements. A data element, Y, in a data group, D, is functionally dependent on another data element, X, in the same data group if for every value of X there is only one corresponding value of Y. X is also called a key. The key of a data group can consist of multiple data elements. Complete functional dependency obtains if a dependent data element depends on all the data elements of the key and not just on a subset of them. It is possible to have multiple keys in a data group; such additional keys are called candidate keys. A data group is in the second normal form if the following conditions hold:

1. The requirements of the first normal form are met.

2. Every non-key data element is completely functionally dependent on a key or candidate key.

The second condition above is not yet fulfilled in the example. The data group for the detail line has a key consisting of the invoice number, the billing period, the personnel number and the program. The data element, hours, depends on the entire key. The data elements, name and fee, however, depend only on the personnel number. This could result in redundant storage of the name and fee information because the same values for these data elements might occur in many detail lines.

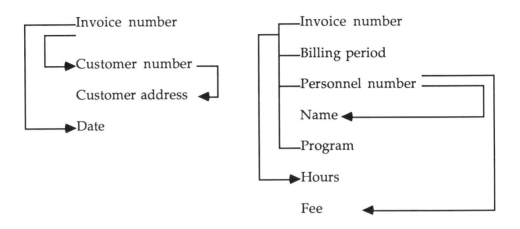

Figure 5.5: Data elements in the first normal form

In order to eliminate this problem the data group is transformed into the second normal form. This is accomplished by removing the partial dependencies through splitting of the data group. In this way the data groups shown in Fig. 5.6 are evolved. In these data groups all non-key data elements are completely functionally dependent on their keys.

5.2.3 The Third Normal Form

Data groups in the second normal form sometimes exhibit a problem which can result in processing complications. It is possible for data elements to exist which are not keys but upon which other data elements nevertheless depend. This situation is known as transitive dependency. One of the data groups shown in Fig. 5.6 exhibits this property. The data element, customer address, depends on the customer number. The customer number in turn depends on the invoice number. The customer number is in this case not a proper key because it does not determine the other data elements of the data group (the same customer can occur in many invoices). The customer address here is transitively dependent on the invoice number. This type of transitive dependency can result in dysfunctional redundancies in the storage of data and should, therefore, be

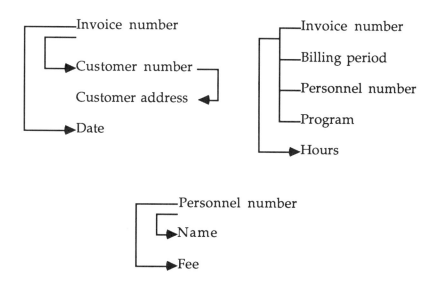

Figure 5.6: Data elements in the second normal form

eliminated. The transformation of the data group into the third normal form by splitting solves the problem. All the data groups shown in Fig. 5.7 are now in the third normal form.

These data group structures represent the optimal way of storing the invoice data. The various groups can be combined in any desired fashion without causing logical inconsistencies. It also turns out in practice that data groups in the third normal form require less storage space and can be more easily maintained. Extendability and clarity are additional important advantages. The three stages of the normalization process are summarized in Fig. 5.8.

5.2.4 The Elimination of Redundancies

The systems designer must go through all the screens and lists of the planned system and normalize the data groups contained therein. This will result in numerous normalized data groups. It will turn out that many lists and screens use the same or very similar data groups. These data groups must be consolidated and integrated. During this process it is incumbent

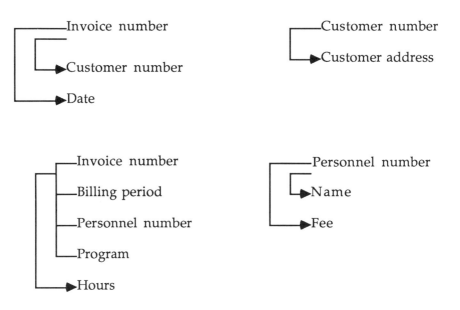

Figure 5.7: Data elements in the third normal form

upon the systems designer to recognize which data elements in the different user views are the same. In such cases the data element name must be standardized. After that has been accomplished, all data groups having the same key are put together. In this way the many data groups that resulted from the normalization process are integrated into a relatively small number of data groups which together constitute the database of the new information system. Since the keys relate to entities or a combination of entities, a database emerges which is based on the principle of entity relationships.

We can better illustrate the process for eliminating redundancies by considering an example. Let us assume that the previous example of an invoice belongs to an organization which also maintains a customer master file. The screen for maintaining this file is shown in Fig. 5.9. If the data elements of this screen are compared with the customer data group of Fig. 5.7, it is immediately obvious that both data groups contain similar data elements which can be integrated. Both data groups have the customer number as key; that indicates that each of them describes attributes of the

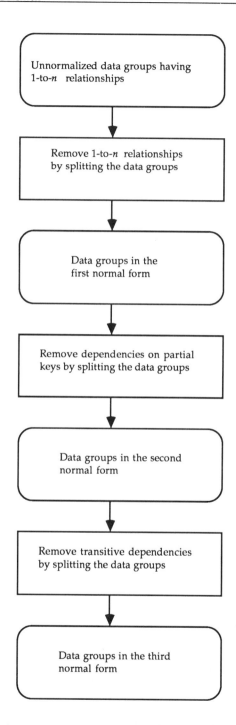

Figure 5.8: The steps of data normalization

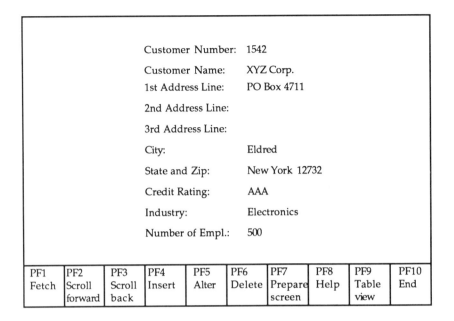

Figure 5.9: Screen for the maintenance
of a customer file

entity, customer. There are, however, a number of differences. The
customer address of the invoice corresponds to several data elements in
the screen layout. There are also data elements in the screen layout which
do not occur at all in the invoice. The two data groups can, nevertheless, be
combined to form the consolidated data groups shown in Fig. 5.10.

5.3 Updating the New System Concept

The result of the processes of data normalization and elimination of
redundancies is a database consisting of data groups in the third normal
form. Each data group should be recorded in the SIABA database as a new
document in the document file. These new documents also have
relationships to certain screen layouts and lists which are already stored as
documents in the document file. These relationships must be recorded by
updating the source document file. The lists will generally have one of the

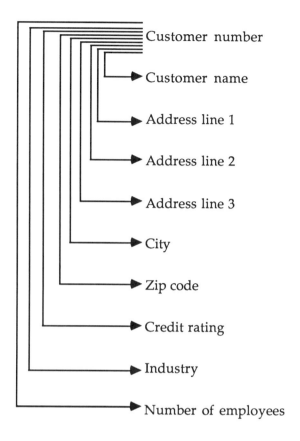

Figure 5.10: Consolidated data group
for customer information

data groups as a source document. The screen layouts will often (but not always) be source documents of other documents.

In Section 4.3.1 a convention was described which limits the function of each program module to the production of a single screen or list. A result of adhering to this convention is that the document file in combination with the source document file, now defines the relationships between all the programs and data groups of the system. This makes it possible to generate system flow diagrams automatically. An example of such a system flow diagram is illustrated in Fig. 5.11.

In this stage of the development of the data model there is only one data group for each key in the system. The entire data group is accessed by

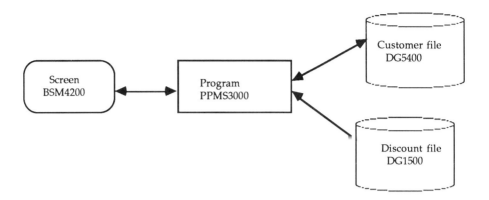

Figure 5.11: Example of a system flow diagram

every program that uses any of the data elements in that group. Many programs, however, use only a subset of the data elements of the data groups they access. That could cause certain problems. The document/source document relationships, for example, are not precise enough to support the generation of a program/data element cross reference. Moreover, programs have access to data elements which have nothing to do with their legitimate functions, a fact that can result in data security problems. For these reasons the principle of data starvation should at some later stage be applied. This involves creating record layouts for the programs which contain only those data elements that are absolutely necessary. These layouts are then added to the document and source document files. This refinement should only be done, however, after the prototype has become stable because a multiplicity of record layouts for the same logical data group make the maintenance of the test environment much more complex.

The generation of the system's flow diagrams is the last step in the definition of the proposed system prototype. All screen layouts, lists, programs and data groups are now designed and documented in the SIABA database. The prototype system design is complete; the prototype can now be constructed using the standard program modules.

Table 5.2: Seminar registration

Code number of seminar: _____

Seminar title: _____

Date and location of seminar   2 Oct. 91 - New York   ☐
                                9 Oct. 91 - New York   ☐
                                3 Oct. 91 - Chicago   ☐
                                6 Oct. 91 - Chicago   ☐
                                6 Nov. 91 - Dallas   ☐
                                7 Nov. 91 - Dallas   ☐

Participants:

Family name: _____ First name: _____

Position:_____ Department: _____

Company: _____

Street/PO box: _____

City: _____

Telephone: _____

Family name: _____ First name: _____

Position:_____ Department:_____

Company: _____

Street/PO box: _____

City: _____

Telephone:_____

5.4 Review Questions and Exercises

1. What are the problems associated with insular system solutions?

2. What should be the basis for the organization of information and why?

3. List the most important principles for defining data elements.

4. What is data independence?

5. Table 5.2 shows a registration form for a seminar. Design a corresponding data model in the third normal form.

5.5 Notes

[1]W. R. Durell, *Data Administration*, New York: McGraw-Hill, 1985, p. 79.
[2]W. R. Durell, *Data Administration*, New York: McGraw-Hill, 1985, p. 42.

6 Building the Prototype

The second, fourth and fifth chapters discussed the first phase of the three phase method. This first phase consists of the analysis of the current system and the development of a proposal for a new system. After completion of the first phase the new information system is defined and must either be acquired in the form of a software package or constructed using the standard modules described in Chapter 3. If the new information system is to be implemented in the form of a software package, the activities of the second phase are limited to the selection and installation of the appropriate products. In order to reach a well-founded decision, each candidate software package should be considered as part of an alternative enterprise model. The system designer should attempt to integrate the screens, lists and data structures of each package into the SIABA model in exactly the same way as with an in-house development. That means that each input and output of the package under consideration should be mapped into the jobs and tasks affected. By doing that the changes in work procedures that the implementation of the package is going to necessitate will become visible. The potential savings and additional costs (= negative savings) for each task should also be ascertained and recorded. On the basis of this information a cost/benefit analysis for each alternative package can be generated. The alternative with the greatest net benefit is the software package to choose.

The installation of the package is then a relatively simple matter because the division of labour among users has been defined in the SIABA model and the technical details can be handled by the vendor.

In the case of an in-house development the execution and coordination of the activities of the second phase are more complex. Here it is necessary to modify, compile and test a relatively large number of program modules. There are many ways that these tasks can be grouped and scheduled; some are much better than others. A well-planned sequencing of the programming activities can reduce the costs of this phase (particularly the cost of testing) quite dramatically. For this reason it is important to work out a precise plan for the construction of the prototype.

This plan should then be used to guide the process of fitting the standard program components together and testing the system. By adhering to a carefully devised programming sequence, the effort of constructing the test environment will be minimized. In addition, there are certain measures for the maintenance of the test environment that speed up testing and make it more reliable. This chapter explains how to make a plan for the software development activities of phase two and how to manage the processes of programming and testing.

6.1 Planning Phase 2

6.1.1 Estimating Costs

If the proposed system is going to be implemented in the form of a software package, the main cost component in the second phase will be the price of the package. Very often the costs of the technical installation are included in the price. Most software vendors provide some limited initial assistance for free but charge extra for more extensive support. In almost all cases a maintenance fee is required which is usually about 15 per cent of the purchase price per year. It is a good idea to request from the vendor in writing a realistic estimate of total costs for the first five years of operation based on the experience of other users of the product.

Table 6.1: Programmer's time sheet

Time sheet

Programmer: Mustermann, G.   Personnel No.: 4711

Time Period: 3 APR. 91 - 9 APR. 91

Date	From Time	To Time	Hours	Project	Program	Type
3 APR. 91	8:00	17:00	8.0	ABZ	AB4000	3
4 APR. 91	8:00	12:00	4.0	ABZ	AB4000	3
4 APR. 91	13:00	17:00	4.0	ABZ	AB4020	2
5 APR. 91	8:00	17:00	8.0	ABZ	AB4020	2
6 APR. 91	8:00	17:00	8.0	ABZ	AB4020	2
7 APR. 91	8:00	17:00	8.0	ABZ	AB4020	2

Total: 40.0

In the case of an in-house development the cost of the second phase depends on the number and type of program modules required. Because different program modules exhibit different degrees of complexity, a different cost factor is used for each component type. The fourth chapter discussed the way cost calculations are automated in the SIABA system. This process requires a standard cost table which stores a costing factor for each program type. The standard costing factors can vary quite significantly depending on the characteristics of the development environment and the quality of the programmers and the reusable program modules. For this reason it is appropriate to base the costing factors on empirical experience and to adjust them at periodic intervals. This is accomplished by keeping a time record of programming activities for every project such as the one illustrated in Table 6.1. This document records the actual work time needed for the development and testing of each program. At regular intervals the time sheet data should be summarized and compared with the estimates stored in the SIABA database. The results of the comparisons can then be used to adjust the values of the standard costing table. In this way the basis for cost estimation will be improved with every project.

6.1.2 Determining the Programming Sequence

Most bottlenecks experienced in programming projects result from problems with testing. This is particularly the case using the SIABA method since the actual programming is especially easy owing to the use of reusable modules. The programmer´s most significant effort, therefore, consists in making certain that programs function properly. One of the reasons why this activity takes up so much time is that the programmer usually has to construct a realistic test environment before a proper test can be performed. Specifically this means storing records in various files before actually testing the program. This often involves many records and enormous amounts of labour just to deduce what might be realistic contents for the records. In order to store the records, some kind of data entry programs must be available. These data entry programs can either be components of the application system or programs written expressly for testing purposes (so-called scaffolding). If additional programs must be written just for test purposes, that, of course, increases the development costs of the system. It is, therefore, appropriate that the sequence of programming be planned in such a way that the recording and maintenance of test data can be performed as much as possible using the database maintenance modules of the applications system. That has three advantages:

1. Fewer programs must be written.

2. The testing is more realistic because the test data originate in the same way they will in practice.

3. The database maintenance programs get tested very thoroughly.

To achieve these advantages the programming sequence should be determined by the network of logical information flows. That means that the first programs to be written are the programs that record the data of the primary documents. After that the rest of the programs are written in the sequence of the logical transformations. In this way it becomes possible to set up the necessary test environment for each module test using already existing system components. An example will help clarify this procedure. Fig. 6.1 shows a flow chart of a system used to maintain the operational data of a training institute. This institute conducts seminars at different education centres with different schedules. Schedules for the seminars are worked out several times a year and published. Clerks receive registrations from participants and record them in a file. The recording of the registrations causes the generation of debits into a accounts receivable file. These, in turn, result in the creation of invoices that are sent to the companies of the participants. When the invoices are paid, the payments are recorded in the accounts receivable file as credits.

The files in Fig. 6.1 are depicted in the sequence of the logical information flows. In order to minimize the effort required for writing scaffold programs the programs in this diagram should, therefore, be written from left to right. Before the scheduling program can be tested, for example, a course file, an instructor file, a education centre file, a term file and a calendar file must exist. For this reason it would make sense to write the corresponding file maintenance programs before the scheduling program. (The sequence of the programming of these file maintenance programs can, however, be arbitrary.) The same basic principles apply for all the rest of the programs of the system.

6.1.3 Scheduling the Programmers

One of the errors most frequently made in software development projects is the use of too many programmers. This usually happens because anxiety

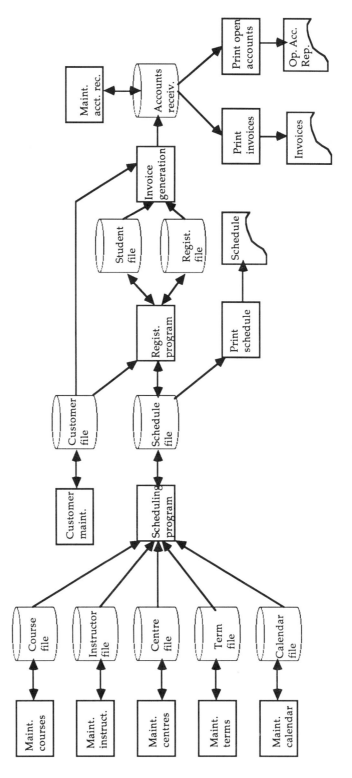

Figure 6.1: System flow diagram for training institute

about meeting delivery deadlines induces managers to assign additional programmers to the project. For a number of reasons, however, this turns out to be very inadvisable. The law of diminishing returns is nowhere more in evidence than in programming. This has to do with the fact that changes in the data model during the programming phase are practically inevitable in every software project. Such changes have to be coordinated with all the programmers participating in the project. The more programmers involved, the more time is required for coordination discussions. With a large number of programmers it is altogether possible that more time is spent communicating than programming! For this reason an old rule of thumb says that the marginal utility of the fifth programmer in a project team is equal to zero. Moreover, the quality of the system suffers from the participation of an excessive number of programmers. A good system exhibits conceptual integrity, i.e. all routines are constructed according to the same principles. The more programmers there are involved, the more difficult it is to achieve this conceptual integrity. The best efforts at standardization cannot guarantee programming homogeneity if too many programmers with different programming styles participate in the development. For these reasons two rules should be observed when scheduling programmers:

1. The number of programmers assigned to the project should be kept to the absolute minimum that still allows completion within the desired time frame. When in doubt, use fewer rather than more programmers. Never succumb to the temptation to assign more programmers to a late project - it will only get later.

2. The division of labour among the programmers should be organized in a way which minimizes their communication requirements. That is best accomplished by assigning each programmer a subsystem which is relatively complete in itself, i.e. a unit of software that has a relatively small number of well-defined interfaces to other subsystems.

These principles can be illustrated by considering the system shown in Fig. 6.1. The ideal situation would be if all thirteen of these programs could be taken over by a single programmer. If time requirements dictate that two programmers have to be employed, additional costs will be inevitable because the programmers are bound to hinder each other's progress in certain ways. One programmer, for example, would probably write the first six programs up to and including the program which maintains the schedule file; the other programmer would take over the rest of the programs. The interface would then be the schedule file. The second programmer could only begin his/her work after a scaffold program to create test data for the schedule file had been written. This program would be thrown away after completion of the project. In addition, delays would come about every time a change in the format of the schedule file became necessary because these changes would have to be discussed and the scaffold program adjusted accordingly. These kinds of communication problems grow geometrically with the number of programmers involved.

6.1.4 Setting up a Critical Path Network

One very powerful technique for dealing with projects of all kinds and sizes (not just software projects) involves the use of critical path networks. For years this technique was limited to large, complex engineering projects because of the considerable overhead required for setting up and maintaining the networks in batch software environments. The mouse-oriented, graphical user interfaces available on today's microcomputers have made network planning feasible for even the smallest of projects. Such user interfaces make it possible to record, alter, store and print out network information very easily using interactive graphics. The stored data can typically be displayed and printed in many different formats. PC-based network planning systems have become one of the most convenient ways to control projects.

Projects are executed to achieve particular concrete results. In network planning the availability of a result or a group of results is referred to as a milestone. The project has been completed when all milestones are available. In order to achieve the milestones certain activities - usually in a particular sequence - must be completed. The milestones, the activities and the logical relationships among them are depicted graphically in a critical path network.

To illustrate a critical path network we shall use the activities and milestones that would be involved in the development of the training system shown in Fig. 6.1. It is assumed that two programmers are to be assigned to this project.

The system consists of three subsystems:

1. The scheduling system.
2. The registration system.
3. The invoicing system.

In order that the programmers have about the same number of programs to work on, one of them is allocated the scheduling system and the other the registration and invoice systems. The project has five milestones: the project start, the availability of the scheduling system, the availability of the registration system, the availability of the invoicing system and the project end. The first step in the development of a planning network is the creation of a graphic representation of the milestones in the order in which they are to be completed. The milestones are depicted in Fig. 6.2 as rounded boxes. This diagram indicates that the activities for achieving the milestone 'scheduling system' happen parallel to the activities for achieving the milestones 'registration system' and 'invoicing system'. The activities for the registration system and the invoicing system, however, must take place in series; first the registration system is developed, then the invoicing system. In this way a network determines the logical sequence of activities in a project, i.e. which activities can run currently and which can only happen after certain other activities have been completed.

The next step in the development of a critical path network consists in filling out the milestone network with the activities needed to achieve

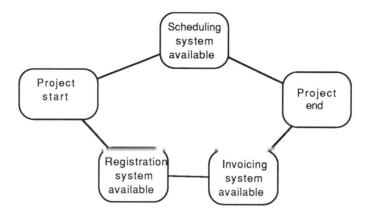

Figure 6.2: Milestones of training system

the milestones. Activities are usually represented as square boxes such as those shown in Fig. 6.3. In the example, almost every activity involves the writing and testing of a program. Since two programmers are assigned to the project, there are two parallel paths of activities which run concurrently and are relatively independent of each other. The serial order of the activities in each path indicates that the programs referred to are to be written and tested one after the other. The sequence is primarily determined in this case by the logical relationships of the various files. In the upper path of this diagram the sequence of programs is arbitrary and could be arranged differently by the scheduler; the only reason for the serial sequence in this instance is the fact that a programmer usually only works on one program at a time. This, however, is the exception rather than the rule in critical path networks.

Occasionally logical dependencies exist between certain activities in two parallel paths. That means that a particular activity in one path cannot begin even though its predecessor activity in the same path has been completed. It must wait until another activity in a different path has taken place. In this case the activity in the second path is also a logical predecessor of the first activity. This relationship is expressed by a line connecting the two activities. In the example there is only one example of this kind of

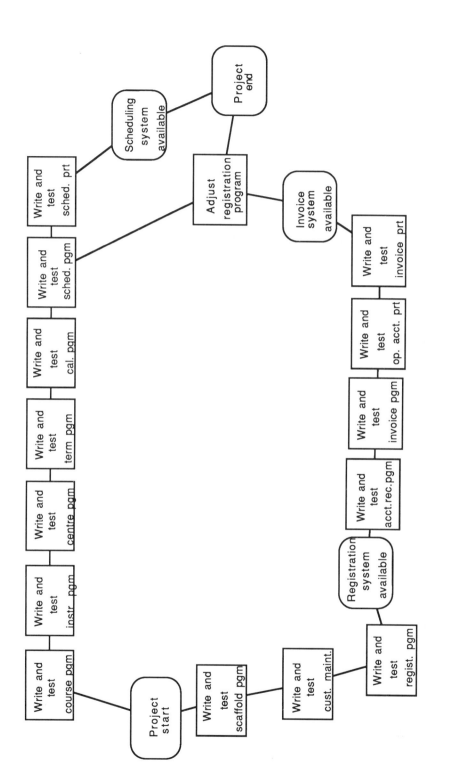

Figure 6.3: Planning network for training system

constraint. The second programmer has to complete an activity called 'adjust registration program' because the schedule file was created for test purposes by a scaffold program. It only makes sense to start that activity after the activity 'write and test schedule program' has been completed. This example has, of course, been simplified for learning purposes; in real-life projects critical path networks typically have many such constraints.

In order to achieve the most important benefits of a planning technique only two more pieces of information must be stored for each activity: the duration and the responsible person or work group. After that, a start date is entered for the entire project. On the basis of this information the network software can then produce a variety of useful reports and graphics. The earliest start and finish dates, for example, can be calculated automatically for every activity taking the logical relationships and durations of the other activities into consideration. As part of this process the critical path through the network is determined; that is the path on which the delay of any activity will cause the delay of the project end date. (The programs on this path should definitely be assigned to the best programmer available.)

In Fig. 6.4 the network is shown once again, this time with the earliest start dates, the durations and the programmers responsible shown. The earliest start date appears on the upper left-hand side of each box. To the right of it is the duration in days. A project start date of 1 Jun. 89 was input and the network software calculated a project end date of 30 Jun. 89. (The system assumed a five day work week and took non-working days such as holidays into consideration.) All the earliest start dates were calculated by the software on the basis of the project start date, the durations and the logical relationships among the activities.

The system also worked out the critical path, which in Fig. 6.4 is the lower one shown in bold. The upper path has a slack of four days. That means that the first programmer will have finished four days before the second programmer. The constraint between 'write and test scheduling program' and 'adjust registration program' has no effect on the project end date in this case because the first programmer is going to be finished much earlier than necessary.

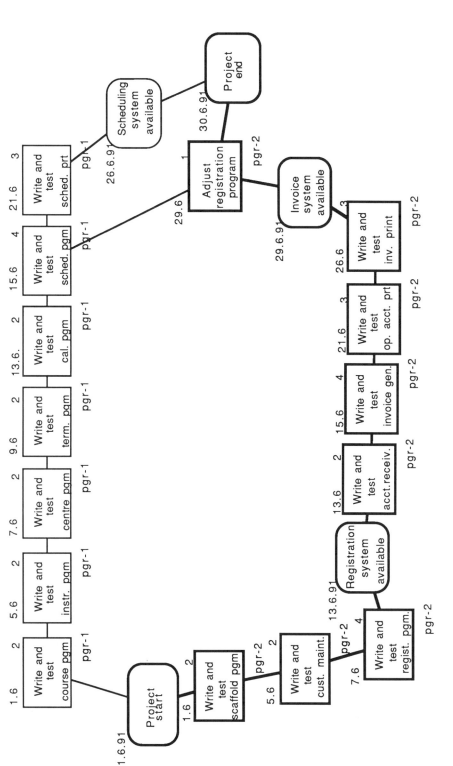

Figure 6.4: Planning network with dates

A critical path network offers an outstanding overview of the activities of a project. Having such an overview available is a great help both in the planning and execution of the project. The network shown in Fig. 6.4, for example, makes it immediately obvious that a possibility exists for shortening the overall project duration. Since the first programmer is going to be finished four days before the other, he/she could take over one of the print programs of the invoice system. That could theoretically cut a day off the project. In practice, however, it is hardly worth while in this case because the communication effort would probably involve more than the day saved. Another interesting piece of information which the network provides is that the activity 'adjust registration program' can be started any time after 21 Jun. 91. That means that the second programmer is free to write his/her last three programs in any desired order.

Fig. 6.4 shows only three pieces of information per activity: the earliest start date, the duration and the programmer responsible. The system maintains, however, a variety of other information elements which can be called up as desired; these include the latest start date, earliest end date and latest end date. Most critical path network systems can display and print their information in several different formats. The bar chart illustrated in Fig. 6.5, for example, shows another way of displaying the network data. Many systems also provide additional features such as cost control, resource allocation, etc., which cover almost every aspect of project planning. In data processing projects, however, the network itself usually turns out to be the most useful planning instrument.

A critical path network is very useful during the execution of the project. It is advisable to give each participant a copy of the network at the start of the project. This helps to make it clear to everyone how important each individual deadline is to the overall project schedule. As activities are completed in the course of the project, the planned dates in the network should be replaced by actual dates. If the actual dates are input into the system, a new network can be generated which shows the consequences of any delays. The network also shows very clearly who was responsible for the delays. This kind of information is indispensable for good project management.

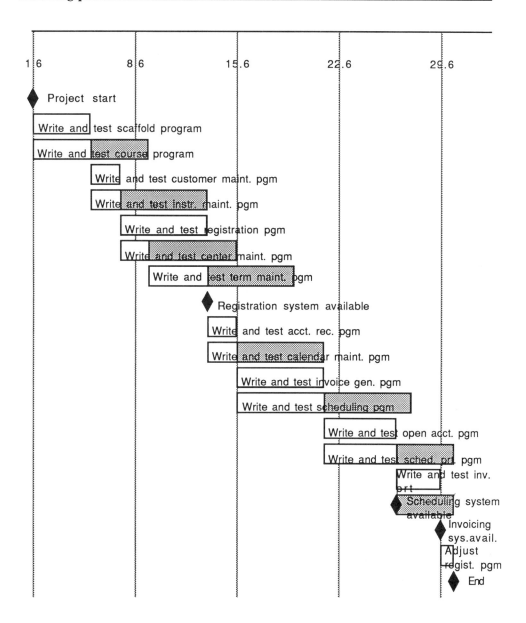

Figure 6.5: Bar chart for training system

6.2 The Importance of Reusable Components

It was pointed out in the first chapter that the use of reusable components is one of the most effective productivity strategies for efficient software development. Reusability is achieved by standardizing all programs and program components and making these standardized components available to the programmers in a central component library. In addition, the programmers need certain tools in order to be able to form the components effectively into finished application functions. It is also necessary that the finished programs be subjected to rigorous quality control which among other things ensures that the standard components have been properly used. The degree of success of a reusability strategy depends, therefore, on the characteristics of the reusable library, the appropriateness of the tools used and the thoroughness of quality control.

6.2.1 The Central Component Library

The most important components in the reusable library are the twelve basic model programs. It is very important that these models be executable programs and not just empty frames. The programmer should have the opportunity to run the programs in their original forms because this makes it easier to localize problems when testing the altered versions. The model programs should exhibit an intermediate level of difficulty; a model that is too simple does not cover enough of the features that will be required in real life; a model that is too complex will require an excessive amount of alteration effort. All models must, of course, exhibit a very high level of technical expertise because any weaknesses will propagate themselves throughout the entire installation.

The model programs themselves consist of components which should be standardized and stored in the central library. Examples of standard components are shown in Table 6.2. All other routines which are used in many programs should, whenever possible, be parameterized, standardized and stored in the central component library.

Table 6.2:   Contents of the component library

- Basic model programs

- Screen input and output routines

- Database access routines

- Table access routines

- Subroutines for converting dates

- Subroutines for string manipulation

- Statistical and mathematical subroutines

- Company-specific routines for such things as
  tax calculations, ageing of accounts, etc.

The basic model programs as well as all subcomponents must be well documented. The best way to do this is to establish a standardized documentation format which is included in the source code as comment lines. The documentation of each module should contain a description and an alteration guide. Both should be updated immediately whenever the source code is changed. This is the best way to guarantee that the documentation always remains accurate. It also makes it possible to generate a handbook automatically from the contents of the central component library. The print routine used for this purpose should be able to create a detailed table of contents in addition to the handbook. Every programmer should always have an up-to-date copy of the handbook available.

It is advisable to assign the maintenance of the central library to a particular employee. This employee is responsible for the establishment of standards, the maintenance of the library and the technical support of the programmers. S/he should be the only one allowed to update the library;

all others should be limited to read-only access. This employee will play a key role in all development projects and should, therefore, be extremely well-qualified. S/he should also be well-integrated into the process of quality control.

6.2.2 Tools for Building the Prototype

The most important tool for programming is the source code editor. Every programmer spends a great proportion of his or her working life manipulating source code. For this reason it is essential that the best available editor be used. In addition to the basic functions a good editor should have the following features:

1. Full screen maintenance of the source code. (Line editors should by now be a thing of the past.)

2. The ability to copy blocks of text both within the file being edited as well as from and to other files.

3. Concurrent editing of several files (split screen editing).

Considering that the above features have long been the state of the art, it is quite incredible that so many editors on the market still do not have them. If a decent editor does not come with the operating system in use, then the acquisition of an appropriate package should be the first order of business.

The second most important tool in programming is a debugger. The debugger should make it easy to execute a program or any part of a program one instruction at a time. During this process it should be possible to examine the contents of variables and change them if desired. The absence of a good debugger can lengthen the time required for testing by whole orders of magnitude.

In the same way that a debugger gives a programmer control over internal data during testing, another tool must provide the same type of control over external data (files, databases, etc.). Most database management systems offer some kind of query language with which data can be stored, listed or deleted. Other data structures rely on utilities, generators or user-written procedures. In any case every programmer will need to be able to create data records as part of a test environment before testing can begin. After each test s/he will need to be able to display the data and see if all changes have happened as desired. The importance and the time necessary for such activities are usually underestimated. It is altogether possible that a programmer spends two hours writing a program and then needs two days to test it. Most of the test effort typically has to do with building and rebuilding the test environment and monitoring its transformation during the various stages of testing. An efficient tool for the maintenance of test environments can, therefore, have an enormous impact on programmer productivity while at the same time improving quality by encouraging more thorough testing. It is very rare to find a data processing installation that has solved this problem adequately.

In the development of interactive programs much time is spent designing and coding screen layouts. The time needed for this task can be significantly reduced through the use of a screen generator. A good screen generator enables the design of a screen as a simple text matrix, the easy allocation of program variables to the screen and the automatic generation of any data definition statements needed by the program. A good product also provides documentation for the screen layout. The documentation should include a snapshot of what the user sees, a comprehensive overview of the program variables involved and an easy-to-understand mapping of the variables to the screen fields.

A fifth category of tools has to do with the interface between applications programmers and systems programmers. In the world of large mainframe computers, applications programmers writing interactive and/or database applications cannot usually complete their work without the assistance of systems programmers.

Table 6.3: The most important tools for software development

- Modern, full-screen source code editor

- Debugger

- Tool for maintaining and viewing test environments

- Screen generator

- Tools for processing systems parameters

The applications programmers must provide the systems programmers with certain information about their new programs so that various parameters of the operating system can be adjusted accordingly. Examples from the IBM world include such things as transaction codes, program control blocks, program status blocks, etc. Since systems programming on large mainframes has developed into a complex area of knowledge with many separate specialities (with an accompanying bureaucracy of specialists), the interface between application programming and systems programming can become a serious bottleneck in systems development. It frequently happens, for example, that an application programmer is held up for hours or even days waiting for some small but essential adjustment to a system parameter, an adjustment that only a particular systems specialist is authorized to make. The delays are usually not necessary but only occur because the systems specialist is not aware of the urgency of the change or because the cooperation between the two groups has not been organized efficiently. These kinds of problems can be alleviated by appropriate tools that support the recording of systems requests by application programmers and the subsequent processing of the requests by the systems programmers. Such tools also allow better control of the efficiency of the whole process. If appropriate tools are not available for a given environment, then one should at least develop a well-organized set of procedures to cope with the problem.

6.2.3 Quality Control

All efforts at standardization will come to nothing if the application of the standards is not monitored and controlled. Merely announcing the standards is not sufficient because there will always be some programmers who will try to circumvent them. The proper and consistent application of standards must, therefore, be rigorously enforced by quality control procedures. To support good quality control there should be four types of program libraries (Fig.6.6):

1. The library of reusable software components which is maintained by a designated administrator.

2. A development library which the programmers use to construct and test their modules.

3. A test library in which the finished programs are stored while they are being tested by the users.

4. A production library which contains the programs which have been completely tested and approved.

In phase 2 programs are constructed in the development library using the components from the reusable component library. After a successful program test the programmer informs the library administrator that the module is now ready for user testing. At this point the administrator must check that all standards have been properly adhered to. (This process is easier if all standard routines are stored as separate copy books with dedicated names and the copy books are not physically copied into the programs but called up using a copy verb.) Only after having

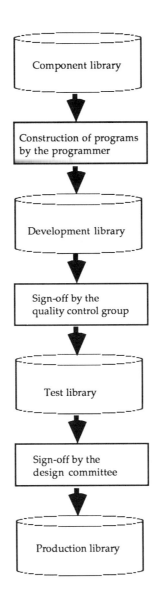

Figure 6.6: Stages in the development of a software system

made certain that the module has been constructed in accordance with
current standards should the administrator copy the module into the test
library. The users then test the program using the procedures for

iterative improvement discussed in the next chapter (phase 3). After this procedure has been completed, the functional accuracy of the software is confirmed in writing by a design committee and all programs are copied into the production library. In this way the quality of the software is verified twice, once by the library administrator with regard to adherence to technical standards and once by the design committee with regard to overall functionality.

6.3 Test Management

The proper organization of test management is a source of productivity gains which is frequently overlooked. In mainframe software development environments, programmers typically spend a surprisingly small proportion of their time actually programming; most of their time by far is spent testing. In most data processing departments the modalities of program testing are left entirely up to the individual programmer, a fact which usually results in inadequate testing of most of the programs. That, in turn, causes embarrassing and time-consuming problems during the process of iterative improvement and has a negative effect on the confidence of users in the technical competence of the software developers. The most common reasons for this problem are the following:

1. There are usually not enough realistic test data readily available.

2. The maintenance of a good test environment is too difficult.

3. The programmers get in each other's way trying to use the same test environment for different purposes.

All three problems can be significantly alleviated by careful organization and management of testing (Table 6.4).

Table 6.4: Requirements for efficient test management

- Well-coordinated testing plans

- Sufficient quantities of realistic test data

- Tools for the maintenance and display of test data files

- Procedures for restoring test environments after changes

6.3.1 Organizing Test Data

The development of test data should under no circumstances be left up to the individual programmer because programmers always test their programs with data which correspond to their own expectations about the users´ environment. It is not surprising, therefore, that the programs usually work properly with these data because the program logic was specifically designed to handle such cases. Most problems arise, however, because of data constellations that the programmers did not expect. This is the kind of data that must be included in the test environment. For this reason it is very important that someone other than the programmers be responsible for the compilation of test data. The project manager and the users should be intimately involved in the process.

The development of the test data should take place before the corresponding programs are begun. Ideally, actual data should be gathered from the users by the project manager and slightly altered if necessary for security reasons. It is useful for this purpose to develop forms which resemble the screen layouts (photocopies of the layouts usually suffice). These forms are then passed to the appropriate users with the request to fill in a specified number of realistic cases. In the case of table data it is advisable to collect all currently valid entries. In the case of other data groups the required number of cases depends on the variability of the data.

If there are many different possible permutations and combinations of the data, then a relatively large number of test cases is necessary (> 100 records). If the data are fairly homogeneous, then a test population of twenty to thirty records will often suffice. One part of the test data collected is placed at the disposal of the programmers, the other part saved for the quality control procedures of the design committee.

6.3.2 Managing the Test Environment

The maintenance of the test environment is fairly simple in the case of batch applications, but somewhat more complex in the case of interactive programs. A typical batch program has input and output files. In the course of a test the program usually reads once through the input file or files and creates the output file or files. The correctness of the processing can easily be determined by comparing the contents of the input and output files. It is possible to repeat the test simply by deleting the output files and starting again. With interactive programs the data files are often altered in place during the course of processing so that the original constellation of data is destroyed. Moreover, every return of the screen can cause changes in the data making it more difficult to track the transformations. A good test should, however, be a strictly controlled experiment in which the states of the data structure before and after every change can be easily determined and documented. In addition, it must be possible to repeat tests as often as necessary with a modicum of effort. These problems can be successfully dealt with by proper organization of test procedures. Procedures must be available with which snapshots of the database contents can be stored, listed and/or restored at will. Before each test is conducted, a copy of the test environment should be made in such a way that the original contents can be reloaded with little effort. It should be possible to store multiple snapshots of different states of the data and to restore whichever one is needed.

6.3.3 Managing the Conflicting Needs of Programmers

Programmers often hinder each other´s progress when they use the same test environment. This problem usually has to do with record layout changes. One programmer discovers that a record layout change is necessary for the transaction s/he is working on. Without the new layout no further progress is possible. The change, however, will also affect a second programmer working with the same data structure. The second programmer has just expended a great deal of effort to create a test environment containing many records in the old format. In many database management systems, changing a record format makes it necessary to delete the old database and generate a new one. That means in order to satisfy the needs of the first programmer, the work of the second programmer is ruined. Either the first programmer has to wait for the change or the second programmer has to rebuild his or her test environment. This is another problem which increases geometrically with an increasing number of programmers.

Unfortunately this problem cannot always be totally eliminated. Some database management systems handle the problem better than others. Almost all DBMS vendors claim to have solved the problem through data independence; these claims often turn out in practice to be grossly exaggerated. Older hierarchical and plex database systems cannot accommodate new fields without rebuilding the whole database. More modern relational databases can usually add fields without disturbing data already stored, but cannot handle length changes for existing fields. Utilities frequently exist for regenerating the databases but careful testing of these utilities often reveal serious faults (e.g. disappearing data). It is incumbent upon the project manager to work out a practical concept for dealing with these kinds of problems prior to the start of testing. If the database management system cannot cope adequately with record layout changes, then there are two approaches for alleviating the problem:

1. Each programmer has a copy of the database which can be altered at will.

2. All record layout change requests are brought to the project manager. At regular intervals (once or twice a day) the database is archived in the old format, deleted and regenerated in the new format. The archived data are then reloaded into the new database with appropriate format changes. If no usable utility routines are available, then custom-built ones must be developed.

The first approach is easy to implement but involves problems later. If programmers work on different copies of a database, the system components have a tendency to grow apart. At the end of the testing much work and additional testing might be necessary to integrate the various versions of the database. There is also the possibility that this approach will involve redundant effort in the building of the test environments if data which could be used by many programmers have to be input by each of them separately. In such cases the second approach is better. It requires, however, more administrative effort on the part of the project manager. S/he has to keep up with the testing plans of the various programmers and see to it that the prerequisites for efficient testing are provided as quickly as possible. S/he must understand the consequences of each test as regards the integrity of the test environment and orchestrate activities in such a way as to minimize disturbances.

6.4 Review Questions and Exercises

1. Describe a scientific approach for selecting a software package.

2. How can standard costing techniques be applied to programming projects?

3. How should the sequence of programming be determined?

4. What are the basic rules for scheduling programmers?

5. What components should be available in the reusable
    component library?

6. List the most important steps for software quality control.

7. What is the main problem in testing and why does it occur?

7 Stepwise Refinement

The last phase of the three phase method consists of the refinement of the prototype developed in the second phase. In this third phase the system is adjusted to meet the detailed needs of the organization. This process requires the broad participation of end users in order to ensure the acceptance and relevance of the system. Phase 3 involves four major tasks:

1. The implementation of the system components and the identification of aspects requiring improvement.

2. The concretization of those improvements which are achievable through the application of information technology.

3. The reaching of a consensus among different users' groups concerning improvement priorities.

4. The limitation of improvements to those which have a solid financial justification.

These tasks have technical, psychological, political and economic aspects. The great variety of problems to be solved usually requires the involvement of a relatively large number of people. Such broad participation, however, always implies the danger of cost overruns. For this reason it is essential to orchestrate participation in such a way that the project stays within its budget. In this chapter the organization, management and operating principles of a design committee are explained; a committee run in a well-controlled fashion in accordance with these principles will achieve superior results within a defined period of time.

7.1 The Design Committee

People starting out in business are often surprised to find out how political large organizations are. In college one is led to believe that business success depends primarily on the ability to come up with correct solutions to problems. One expects that the mere ability to prove the correctness of a suggested solution will be enough to elicit the cooperation of all involved more or less automatically. As every experienced manager knows, nothing could be further from the truth. Coming up with the correct solution to a problem is often a trivial task compared with the effort needed to achieve enough cooperation to implement the chosen solution in a large organization. That is particularly true of information systems because successful implementation is so dependent on the active cooperation of people on many levels of the hierarchy. Keeping all information up to date and consistent is only possible in the long run with the voluntary and enthusiastic support of the people involved. For this reason it is very advisable to implement and refine iteratively an information system with the help of a design committee consisting of representatives of a broad cross-section of the user population.

A representative design committee has a high potential for achieving the necessary cooperation of user groups for two reasons:

1. Because of its professional competence. The representatives of the users' groups are better acquainted with the subtle details of their areas than any data processing expert could ever be, and are able to apply this

knowledge to the improvement of the project. For this reason the final product will fit much better to the tasks at hand.

2. Because of its political legitimacy. Since the users are involved in the design of the information system, it is no longer something foreign imposed from outside, but rather something familiar which they have helped create. This usually causes users to identify better with the new system and its goals and reduces anxieties about possible undesirable consequences of the implemention.

In order to achieve these benefits in practice the design committee must be organized and managed according to certain principles. It is very important, for example, that the design committee be composed of people who really understand the practical details of their work areas.   That usually means that membership should not be limited to managers. Many design committees fail because they have too many chiefs and not enough Indians. The kind of feedback needed from the users for the improvement iterations is very specific and often involves subtle details about the work environment. It is unusual to find a manager who is sufficiently aware of these aspects to be able to make a significant contribution to the refinement process. Managers are most useful in the definition of the strategic considerations already handled in phase 1. In phase 3 it is primarily a matter of fine-tuning the operational details. Here managers can set priorities and resolve otherwise unresolvable conflicts, but in practice have little to do most of the time. It is, therefore, advisable that the majority of design committee members be people who are directly involved in the day-to-day details of the work.

The members of the design committee should be carefully prepared for their tasks. They should understand the basics of data processing from a user's viewpoint and be able to pass this knowledge on to the people they represent. They must be familiar with the operating principles of the design committee and be committed to upholding them in practice. They should be the ones who coordinate all data processing activities in their respective areas during both the development and production phases. They should be responsible for training co-workers, developing user guides and answering users´ questions. They should be encouraged to take an active role in identifying user problems and bringing these to the attention of the design committee. In the final analysis it is the members of the design committee who will determine whether or not the system is a success.

Another important aspect of participative design is the assignment of authority and responsibility. The design committee must take full responsibility for the determination of the system´s interface with users. That is only feasible if the design committee has the authority to make the necessary decisions. That means that the committee must have the final word on all design decisions. Top management should specifically invest the design committee with this power. The systems designer and the technical staff must consider themselves to be a service unit for the design committee, i.e. they do not tell the design committee what to do, but only explain technically feasible alternatives and implement what the design committee chooses. The prototype system resulting from phase 2 is only a first attempt at an information system; the design committee is free to modify it in any desired fashion to meet requirements. The role of the systems designer is to develop design modifications on the basis of feedback from the committee, to present these as suggestions for discussion to the committee and, if accepted, to implement them with the help of the technical staff. The interaction between the systems designer and the design committee is illustrated in Fig. 7.1.

The most important management principle for working with design committees is the strict adherence to a precise time plan. One of the greatest dangers associated with the involvement of a committee in the design process is the possibility of endless discussions. This danger is particularly acute with a prototyping methodology because the possibility of future adjustments to the system often results in a superficial approach to the initial definition of requirements. This can cause serious flaws in the design which must be clarified later by long and costly discussions. A study of ninety firms that used prototype development methods showed, for example, that the two greatest problems were limiting the scope of the system and controlling the refinement process.[1] In order to avoid these

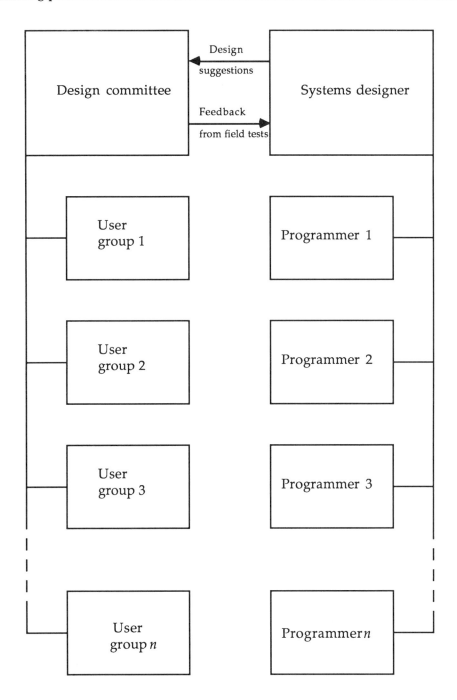

Figure 7.1: The design committee

problems it is necessary to set up a schedule which enables precisely
defined tasks to be finished within a specific time frame. The tasks are
delegated either to the users' coordinators or to the systems designer and
must be completed in the time allotted, even if this involves not
processing all relevant bits of information. The committee meets at regular
intervals (once a week or once every two weeks); every meeting has an
agenda of topics that must be settled in that meeting. The topics generally
have to do with the processing of feedback from specific user areas. A
given user area will normally have only one opportunity during an
improvement iteration to present its suggestions for improvement. These
improvements will then be incorporated in the next release of the
prototype.

The approval of additional improvement iterations depends on
global considerations about the total cost/benefit of the system. That means
that a user area coordinator cannot know if a missed improvement
opportunity can be made up in the future. This circumstance provides a
strong motivation for the user area coordinators to do their homework
thoroughly and punctually.

7.2 Planning Phase 3

In order to cope with their responsibilities successfully the members of the
design committee need a test and implementation plan. The overall plan is
a composite of the plans for the stepwise refinement of each subsystem.
Each planning unit consists of a series of activities which are performed in
a predetermined sequence. A refinement iteration involves one execution
of the activities of a planning unit. These activities illustrated in the
planning network of Fig. 7.2 are as follows:

1. Briefing the coordinator. The first step is to show the user area
   coordinator how to operate those parts of the system for which s/he is
   responsible. After every system change the coordinators must be
   brought up to date.

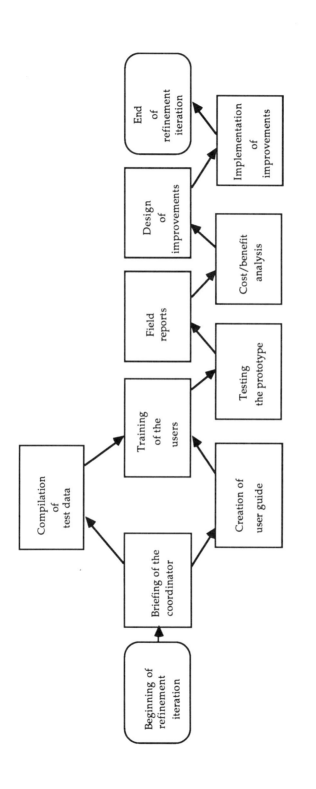

Figure 7.2: Planning network for one refinement iteration

2. Compilation of test data. The user area coordinator must ensure that realistic test data are available.

3. Creation or updating of the user guide. After having been briefed on the operation of the system the user area coordinator must create a user guide with the help of the technical team. The user area coordinator is the right person for this job because s/he speaks the language of the users better than the technical people. Moreover, this is a good opportunity to clarify and elaborate what was learned in the briefing.

4. Training of the users. Once test data and user guides are available, the users are trained by the user area coordinator.

5. Testing the prototype. After having been trained the users test the prototype for a specified period of time using the test data made available to them. The length of the testing period depends on the characteristics of the jobs involved. In any case the testing must continue long enough to go through all relevant work cycles.

6. Field reports. Through discussions with users as well as through his/her own testing the user area coordinator identifies problems in the use of the system and documents them in a report. This report should include an exact description of the tests and illustrate the problems with examples of data.

7. Cost/benefit analysis. The field reports are the basis for discussions in the design committee meetings. Problems and possible solutions are analyzed with respect to achievable benefits. The costs of suggested improvements are compared with the benefits to determine if additional system refinements are worth the effort.

8. Design of improvements. If economically justifiable refinements exist, these are then specified in detail by the committee with the help of the systems designer.

9. Implementation of improvements. After the refinements have been specified in detail, they are implemented by the technical team.

This procedure is followed for every subsystem. Initially two iterations are scheduled for each subsystem. After the activity 'cost/benefit analysis' the iteration is ended immediately if its continuation cannot be economically justified.

The first few design committee meetings are devoted to setting up the test and implementation plan. The iteration procedure described above is the basic building block of the plan. The committee composes the plan with the help of the systems designer by fitting these building blocks together to make a plan for the entire system. The participants responsible for the individual activities must provide time estimates that are then incorporated into the plan. After the completion of two refinement iterations for each subsystem the project is suspended. At this point a critical analysis of the costs and benefits of the entire system is performed once again. The costs of additional refinement iterations are weighed against the possible benefits and a decision is made whether or not it is worthwhile to continue the project. If it is, then the procedure begins all over again. If it is not, the system goes into production as is.

7.3 The Group Design Methods

The activities needed for completing the work described above can be divided into three categories:

1. Investigative activities. The user area coordinators become acquainted with the system and observe it functioning in practice, during which they identify possibilities for improvement.

2. Creative activities. In the design committee meetings the feedback from the field tests is processed in order to evolve suggestions for improvement.

3. Decision-making activities. In the design committee meetings decisions must be made as to whether further refinements of the system are appropriate and, if so, which alternatives will be chosen.

These activities can be facilitated in many different ways. Nigel Cross and Robin Roy have suggested fifteen design methods which can be used for any kind of design project.[2] The correspondence between each of these methods and the three types of project work are shown in Table 7.1. The rest of this section is devoted to explaining the use of each of these methods.

7.3.1 User Trips

With this method the user area coordinator actually takes over the work of a particular user. The coordinator performs the daily tasks of the user and notes any difficulties that arise. S/he also records any interesting details of the work that might have a bearing on the system design. The purpose of this is to acquire a deeper understanding of the specific problems of the job by actively doing the work. This method is particularly appropriate if the users are unable (or unwilling) for any reason to communicate effectively about their experience with the system.

7.3.2 User Research

This method strives to identify user problems through discussion and observation. It is the most common way to find out what is going on in practice. The user area coordinator trains the user in the operation of the system, assigns specific tasks and then observes how the tasks are performed. All problems which arise, as well as improvement suggestions which are made, are recorded in the field report.

Table 7.1: The group design methods (reproduced from Table 1.6)

Design methods	Types of project work		
	Investigative	Creative	Decision-making
User trips	●		●
User research	●		●
Information search	●		
Objective trees	●	●	●
Counterplanning	●	●	
Interaction matrix	●	●	●
Interaction net	●	●	●
Brainstorming	●	●	
Classification	●	●	
Forced connections	●	●	
New combinations	●	●	●
Enlarging the search space		●	
Functional innovation		●	
Performance specification		●	●
Check lists	●		●

7.3.3 Information Search

During all three phases of the project it is necessary to acquire information about the structure and procedures of the organization. In order not to be deluged by an oversupply of information, it is necessary to proceed in a very structured and methodical fashion. Before each research task is performed, specific questions should be worked out for which answers are to be sought within a limited time period. The questions should be formulated in such a way that they can be answered by quantitative information, binary answers (yes/no) or precise, succinct lists. Table 7.2 provides some examples of efficient and inefficient questions. By proceeding in this manner it is possible to reduce the vast amount of information that exists in every organization to a manageable quantity by clearly eliminating those things in which one is not interested. That is particularly important when delegating research tasks (e.g. to user area coordinators) that have to be performed with set time limits. For this reason the method of structured information search is applied very frequently in the building of the SIABA model.

7.3.4 Objective Trees

Empirical studies have clearly established that the explicit formulation of objectives significantly increases the efficiency of any work group.[3] For this reason goal-setting techniques play a major role in many management methods. The objective tree method is a way to analyze goals using top-down decomposition. Global objectives are formulated which are then decomposed into subobjectives. The subobjectives themselves are then further broken down until very specific goals have been identified. This procedure eventually results in a hierarchical, tree-like structure which illustrates the consequences and ramifications of objectives on many different levels. Proceeding in this manner makes it easier to transform sweeping, strategic objectives into concrete, tactical and operational measures that can be achieved in a finite number of steps.

Table 7.2: Sample questions for information search

Inefficient questions	Efficient questions
1. How would you describe your job?	1. Could you divide your typical work day into not more than six major tasks?
2. What information do you need to perform your work?	2. Can you give me a specific example of each document that you use in connection with your work?
3. How would you describe your work load?	3. How many documents do you process in a given time period (day, month, year, etc.)?

As an example of this process, consider an organization that is planning the acquisition of a word processing facility. A brainstorming session has resulted in the identification of the five objectives shown in the upper part of Table 7.3. A closer examination of these objectives reveals that there are really only two major objectives: the creation of business correspondence and the creation and maintenance of software documentation. The other objectives are subobjectives of the two main objectives. This analysis is illustrated in the lower part of Table 7.3 as a tree diagram and as an outline.

A variation of this method can be used to help achieve a consensus about the selection of one of several choices. In this case a detailed objectives' tree is worked out which will be used to judge the merits of the competing alternatives. The objectives on each level of the tree are

Table 7.3: The structuring of objectives

Unstructured objectives for a word processing system

- Business correspondence

- Advertising

- Program documentation

- Diagrams

- Invoices

Structured objectives for a word processing system

Business correspondence   Documentation

 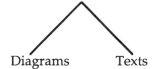

Letters   Advertisements Invoices   Diagrams   Texts

Structured objectives in outline form

1.0 Business correspondence
    1.1 Letters
    1.2 Advertisements
    1.3 Invoices
2.0 Documentation
    2.1 Diagrams
    2.2 Texts

weighted to indicate the relative importance of each objective in relation to the others on the same level. It makes the calculations simpler if the weighting is done in such a way that the weights on any given level always add up to 100.

It is usually not difficult to achieve a consensus in a committee about the abstract structure of the objectives tree and the relative weights of the detailed objectives. Once this has been accomplished, it is possible to evaluate each choice by assigning a score indicating to what degree the choice in question meets the requirements of each objective. This is done by assigning a percentage value to each subobjective on the lowest level of the hierarchy. (For example, 100 per cent would mean that the choice in question completely fulfils the requirements of a particular subobjective.) A total score for a choice is calculated by multiplying the percentage scores for each subobjective by the weighting of that subobjective and summing the products. The choice with the best total score is selected. Each committee member can perform a separate evaluation; the consensus then results from averaging the scores.

This technique can be illustrated using the previous example. Assume that the organization will use the selected word processing system about 70 per cent of the time for software documentation and about 30 per cent of the time for business correspondence. It seems reasonable to use these percentages as the weightings for the two main objectives. The weightings must then be broken down to the most detailed level. Since there are only two levels in our example, this is quite simple. As regards business correspondence, it turns out that the subobjective 'Invoices' is twice as important as the other two subobjectives together. In the area of software documentation the creation of diagrams is the primary requirement. On the basis of these assumptions the evaluation shown in Table 7.4 is performed. In this example the first choice 'loses' despite its good score for the first objective, because of the heavier weighting of the second objective.

To clarify this technique the individual steps are listed once again:

Table 7.4: Structured and weighted objectives
for the acquisition of a word processing system

Objectives	--Weightings--		--Evaluations--			
	Level 1	Level 2	Alt.-1	x Weighting	Alt.-2	x Weighting
1.0 Business correspondence	30					
1.1 Letters		5	100	5	100	5
1.2 Advertisements		5	100	5	50	2.5
1.3 Invoices		20	100	20	50	10
2.0 Documentation	70					
2.1 Diagrams		50	20	10	100	50
2.2 Texts		20	50	10	50	10
Totals:	100	100		50		77.5

1. The objectives on the top level of the objectives tree are assigned a weighting between 1 and 100. All weightings must add up to 100.

2. Each weighting is broken down on the subordinate levels of the hierarchy.

3. For each choice a percentage score is assigned for each subobjective on the lowest level of the tree indicating to what degree that choice satisfies the requirement implicit in the subobjective.

4. Finally, a total score is calculated for each choice by multiplying the percentage scores by the detailed weightings and summing the products.

It should be noted that this is a purely heuristic procedure; both the weightings and the scores are subjective evaluations. Nevertheless, the technique forces the committee members to specifiy explicitly the reasons for their preferences and to think clearly about the relative merits of each choice.

7.3.5 Counterplanning

Counterplanning is a method derived from the dialectic philosophy of Hegel. It is assumed here that truth and progress result from the unification of opposites. To apply this method the design committee first identifies the basic assumptions underlying each design suggestion. It then develops a new set of assumptions by negating the original assumptions and uses this new set of assumptions as the basis for developing a second design alternative. Finally, the committee works out a synthesis of the two alternative designs. The resulting design is not just a mere compromise but rather something which transcends both of the original designs and is recognized by all participants as superior. Counterplanning is very useful in cases where the success of an information system depends on factors (such as the number of transactions to be processed, warehouse turnover, number of service requests, etc.) that cannot be predicted with certainty. By taking widely opposing assumptions into account, the design results in an information system which is more stable and robust.

7.3.6 Interaction Matrix

An interaction matrix is a flexible tool for the graphical representation of the relationships among several factors. Interaction matrices have an almost unlimited number of applications in design technology because of their ability to summarize complex relationships in an easily understandable manner. Interaction matrices are particularly suitable for processing with a computer. Matrices play a major role in the SIABA method (see, for example, the job-task-document matrix, the program/work group matrix, etc.). The decision table illustrated in Table 7.5 is only one special case of an interaction matrix.[4]

7.3.7 Interaction Net

Sometimes the relationships among the elements of a problem are such that they are better represented in the form of an interaction net rather than a matrix. Information flow diagrams, critical path networks and system flow charts are common examples from the information systems area. For many years interaction nets had the disadvantage that their creation and maintenance were rather labour-intensive. In recent years, however, PCs and mouse technology have changed all that. It is now very simple to create and update graphical representations of interaction nets, making their application feasible in more and more areas. The essential products of most CASE systems, for example, consist of various forms of interaction networks.

Table 7.5: Decision table

This decision table is used to calculate income tax amounts, whereby

I = taxable income

T = tax due

Conditions	Rules					
$I > \$640$	●					
$\$640 < I < \$2,440$		●				
$\$2,440 < I < \$17,440$			●			
$\$17,440 < I < \$27,640$				●		
$\$27,640 < I < \$54,640$					●	
$\$54,640 < I$						●
Calculations						
$T = 0$	●					
$T = 0.11\,(I - 640)$		●				
$T = 198 + 0.15\,(I - 2,440)$			●			
$T = 2,448 + 0.28\,(I - 17,440)$				●		
$T = 5,304 + 0.35\,(I - 27,640)$					●	
$T = 14,754 + 0.385\,(I - 54,640)$						●

7.3.8 Brainstorming

Brainstorming is probably the simplest and best known method for stimulating creativity. There are numerous ways to conduct a brainstorming session. The important thing is to avoid negative feedback and destructive remarks. The group should first be presented with a overall description of the problem. The participants are then requested to think up new ideas or approaches to the problem with as little forethought and as spontaneously as possible. Each idea is written onto a blackboard or a card and placed where everyone can see it. Criticism of expressed ideas is strictly forbidden. Improbable or crazy ideas are welcome. The atmosphere should be easygoing and friendly. Ideas once expressed stimulate more and more new ideas in a humorous game of free association. The elements of humour and playfulness are particularly important for the stimulation of creativity. Only after the brainstorming session is over should the ideas be analyzed and a selection made. Brainstorming is very useful for the development of new systems concepts as well as for the generation of alternatives during the refinement iterations.

7.3.9 Classification

The search for meaningful categories for ordering information is one of the most basic activities of every design project. The project environment often appears as a confusing conglomeration of details. In order to proceed the data must first be classified, i.e. divided into categories which adequately express both the similarities and the differences of the detailed information. One way to get started on this process is to note each detail on a card and then to sort and group the cards until recognizable patterns emerge. Categories are then defined to which these patterns can be assigned. The categories should be mutually exclusive and collectively exhaustive. This procedure is often needed in phase in order to group the many activities of a job into a small number of major tasks. In phase 3 it is also frequently necessary for the analysis of test cases. Dividing the attributes of an alternative into advantages and disadvantages is another common application of classification.

7.3.10 Forced Connections

The forced connection method is used to investigate new ways of combining the components of a system. The first step is to create an interaction matrix or interaction net showing the current connections among the systems components. The connections are then simply rearranged and the result analyzed to see if anything useful has evolved. This procedure can be very illuminating because the connections among systems components are often quite arbitrary. Forcing new connections frees the participants from entrenched conceptions and stimulates creativity. This method can be particularly useful in rearranging the information flows of an organization.

7.3.11 New Combinations

This method is similar to the method of forced connections to the extent that both techniques endeavour to find innovative ways to combine system components. In this case, however, one begins by making a list of the major attributes of a system or subsystem. Each of these attributes can usually be achieved in a number of ways. The next step, therefore, is to note all known alternatives for achieving each attribute. Finally all permutations and combinations of the attributes and their alternatives are investigated as regards their feasibility and utility. As an example of this procedure the technical attributes of an information system and some of the possible alternatives are shown in Table 7.6. This matrix representation is known as a morphological chart and helps the designer to overcome the inertia of current conventions. With the help of this list it is easy to see just how many possible combinations there are; in this case there are thirty-six.

Table 7.6: System attributes and alternatives

Attributes	Alternatives
Processing mode	Interactive processing Batch processing
Programming language	Cobol PL/1 Pascal
Hardware	Mainframe Minicomputer Microcomputer
TP-Monitor	CICS SHADOW

Many are unfeasible, but some them will turn out to be useful and innovative.

7.3.12 Enlarging the Search Space

Many design problems arise because of an excessively narrow definition of the problem. This kind of investigative myopia frequently prevents the development of a really innovative solution. For this reason it is often useful to force oneself to enlarge the area of investigation. In the case of information systems it is very common to focus exclusively on the problems of a particular work group or on a given set of procedures. It can happen, for example, that a work group expends enormous efforts to produce a certain piece of information for top management in the belief that this is absolutely essential. It often turns out, however, that the information is not so essential after all and that if top management was informed about the effort involved, it would happily do without it or make do with something else. By extending the investigation to additional work groups (in this case top management) a superior solution is found.

The search space can be too narrow not only with respect to people but also with respect to the types of solutions considered. A tendency always exists to consider current practice as the only feasible model for an information system. This attitude can result in the propagation of existing organizational weaknesses throughout the new information system. It is, therefore, important to force oneself systematically to extend the search space to alternative solutions. There are a number of ways to accomplish this:

1. The solution models of other organizations should be considered; there are always useful things to be learned.

2. Current procedures should always be subjected to a critical analysis. Never stop asking yourself why things are done as they are done and not in some other way.

3. Analogies from different areas should be considered. For example, biological models (cf. neural networks) frequently provide useful analogies for business, electronics or computer science. Even complete fantasies can offer analogies that are useful for the design of an information system.

7.3.13 Functional Innovation

The method of functional innovation helps to find new ways to accomplish the functions of an existing system. The first step is to make a list of the components of the system, together with the functions that each component performs. If known shortcomings exist, these are noted as well. Then one attempts to define new components which perform the same functions but without the shortcomings. This method is particularly appropriate for modernizing an existing information system, for example, when upgrading a system from batch to online. It can also be quite useful for tuning new systems.

7.3.14 Performance Specification

The definition of performance specifications is probably the most important activity in the design process. It involves succinctly describing the system requirements in a way that permits an objective evaluation of the final product. In order not to limit unduly the freedom of the designer the requirements should be formulated in terms of the functionality of the system or subsystem and not presuppose a particular approach to the problem. In other words, a performance specification should determine what the system is supposed **to do** and not what it is supposed **to be**. A performance specification should be on the highest level of generalization that is consonant with achieving the desired results but at the same time be as specific as possible at that level.

7.3.15 Check-lists

Composing a check-list is the simplest design method. A check-list enumerates the criteria that are known to be important in the evaluation of a design. It can serve as a basis for evaluation or simply as a memory aid for the designer. Check-lists have numerous applications in many design methods. Some software design methods are really no more than a collection of check-lists covering various aspects of the design process. Check-lists are a useful means of communication between the design committee and the systems designer because so many issues can be succinctly summarized in this way.

7.4 Need-driven Refinement

The activities of the refinement process are carried out with the help of the fifteen design methods listed in Table 7.1 using the information stored in the SIABA database. The design methods help the participants obtain the necessary detailed information, develop innovative solutions and arrive at rational decisions. The SIABA system particularly supports decision-making by providing a convenient way to compare planned and actual cost and benefits. These data are the basis for the most important activity of each refinement iteration, the analysis of costs and benefits. This analysis determines whether or not the further refinement of a given subsystem is economically justified by the potential marginal benefits. The setting of priorities for project management can also be derived from these data. In this way the project is consistently steered in the direction of the maximization of total net benefits.

7.4.1 The Release Concept

An important prerequisite for the maximization of total net benefits is the avoidance of cost overruns. Cost overruns almost always occur when a system is continuously improved in an ad hoc and uncontrolled fashion. It is then very difficult to maintain an overview of the economics of the project; costs escalate unnoticed. In addition to cost overruns, an uncontrolled approach to improvements causes confusion among the users and makes the maintenance of the documentation more difficult. For these reasons new versions of software systems should be issued as clearly defined editions. A new edition of a software system is generally known as a release. A new release should be numbered and accompanied by a list of the technical characteristics that distinguish it from other releases. The costs and benefits data of each release should also be documented in order to provide an overview of the economic justification of improvements. In order to accomplish this it is useful to archive a copy of the SIABA database which corresponds to each release (the cost/benefit data are the most important aspects in this case).

7.4.2 Processing User Feedback

The efficient refinement of an information system requires the systematic processing of user feedback. Two instruments are especially useful for this purpose, the contents of the SIABA database and the field test report shown in Table 7.7. The first part of the field test report (up to and including the description of problems encountered) is filled out by the user area coordinator after observing the field tests, and provides a basis for discussion in the design committee meeting. During the meeting improvement suggestions are worked out with the help of the system designer. Cost/benefit estimates are developed for both the current version of the system as well as for an improved version. The costs incurred in the testing are recorded in the field 'additional costs' in the document file; the corrected benefit estimates are stored in the task file as actual benefits. On the basis of this information the cost/benefit analysis illustrated in Table 7.8 can be automatically generated, which documents the economics of the current release. After that, a copy of the SIABA database is made in which the cost/benefit data of an improved release are stored. Here again the economics are documented in the form of a cost/benefit analysis. After all this information has been stored for all subsystems, it is easy to decide on the basis of a comparison of the two cost/benefit analyses (one for the existing system and one for an improved version) whether or not further refinement iterations are appropriate. It makes economic sense to continue the refinement process until no further increases in the total net benefits can be achieved. At this point the organization has the economically optimal information system. The refinement iterations should then be discontinued and the information system put into production.

Table 7.7: Field test report

Subsystem or program: _____

_____

Work group or user: _____

_____

Test period: _____ Release number: _____
Description of test environment: _____

_____

_____

Number of test cases: _____
Problems encountered (continue on separate pages): _____

_____

_____

_____

Suggested improvements with cost estimates (continue on
separate pages): _____

_____

_____

_____

Potential benefits per task (continue on separate pages): _____

_____

_____

_____

_____

Total costs of current release: _____
Total benefits of current release: _____
Estimated costs of improved release: _____
Estimated benefits of improved release: _____

| (Date) | (User area coordinator) | (Systems designer) |

Table 7.8: Cost/benefit analysis per work group

WG code	Work group	Share of costs NPV	Add. costs NPV	Estimated benefits NPV	Actual benefits NPV
4711	Stock room	120,000	50,000	150,000	110,000
4712	Sales	500,000	100,000	750,000	750,000
4713	Accounting	80,000	80,000	200,000	200,000
	Totals:	700,000	230,000	1,100,000	1,060,000

7.5 Review Questions and Exercises

1. List the most important tasks involved in stepwise refinement.

2. Why is the use of a design committee an effective way to achieve the necessary cooperation between system developers and user groups?

3. What are the most important principles for the organization of a design committee?

4. List the activities of a refinement iteration.

5. What are the three kinds of activities that a design committee performs?

6. Which design method is appropriate for delegating research tasks? for achieving a consensus about the selection of one of a number of alternatives? For precisely defining system requirements?

7. Why is a release concept useful?

8. How long should the refinement process be continued?

7.6 Notes

[1]J. M. Carey and J. D. Currey, 'The prototyping conundrum', *Datamation*, Vol. 35, No. 11, 1 June 1989, p. 30.

[2]N. Cross and R. Roy, *Design Methods Manual*, Milton Keynes: The Open University Press, 1975.

[3]See, e.g., H. L. Tosi and S. Carroll, 'Management by Objectives' in K. N. Wexley and G. A. Yukl, *Organizational Behavior and Industrial Psychology*, New York: Oxford University Press, 1975.

[4]A decision table consists of three components: the actions or calculations that are to be performed in a particular decision situation, the conditions under which these actions are to be performed and the rules which link each condition with the corresponding action.

8 Summary of the Three Phase Method

The goal of the three phase method is the increase of productivity in all business areas through the application of selected information engineering techniques. The essential elements of the three phase method are enterprise modelling, reusable software components, prototyping and iterative refinement with the help of a user committee. These elements are applied according to the three phase methodology illustrated in Fig. 8.1:

Phase 1. Analysis of the current state of the organization with the help of structured interview techniques. Development of an enterprise model through the use of an interview database. Design of a prototype consisting of twelve reusable model programs.

Phase 2. Creation of the prototype or selection of the software package that best approximates the functionality of the prototype.

Phase 3. Iterative refinement of the information system with the help of a design committee made up of a cross-section of the users. Control of the refinement process by cost/benefit analyses.

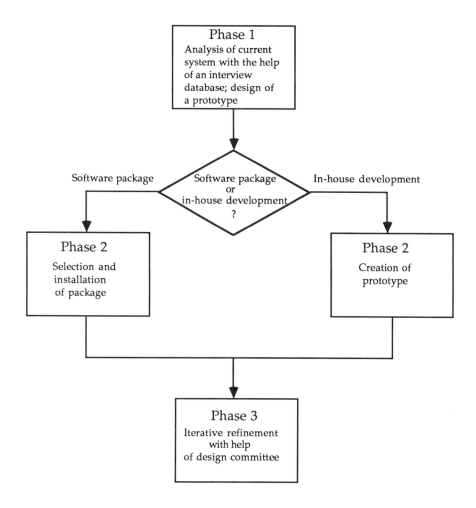

Figure 8.1: The three phase method

Through the application of these techniques it is possible to implement efficient information systems with a predictable amount of effort.

8.1 The Enterprise Model as a Statement of the Current System

One of the key ideas of information engineering is the concept of a holistic approach to systems design. The enterprise is seen as an organic unity; its components acquire their primary significance through integration in the overall, goal-directed entity. In order to be able to comprehend an enterprise in these terms it is necessary to have a model which provides an overview of strategies, structure, procedures and information. A model of this type supports systems planning by illuminating the relationships between the information system and the business organization from the very start. It is appropriate to set up the model in such a way that it is easily updated so that new knowledge can be quickly and continuously taken into account. The information resulting from the analysis of the current state of the organization should, therefore, be stored in the form of a database which serves as a computerized enterprise model. This database records information about the enterprise strategy and structure, problems and possible solutions, objectives and subobjectives as well as the operational procedures and the information that these require. Everything that one needs to know in order to increase organizational efficiency through the use of information systems can be derived from this collection of data.

The information needed to fill the database can be gathered efficiently using structured interview techniques. These techniques call for the collection of specific information elements in a predetermined sequence. The interviewees are briefed beforehand about the content of their interviews so that the required information can be surveyed with a minimum of effort.

Once the data about the current state of the organization are stored in the database, a variety of computerized analyses can be generated, which provide a quantitative basis for setting the priorities of systems design activities. Analyses such as the ABC analysis of potential benefits show which parts of the organization have the greatest savings potential thus enabling a scientific approach to requirements planning. The contents of the interview database record who performs which tasks with the help of what information. On the basis of these data a systems designer can design a prototype information system that closely corresponds to organizational needs.

8.2 The Enterprise Model as a Statement of the Required System

The data structure used to model the current state of the organization can also be used to plan the new system. In a computerized information system manually created sources of information are replaced by screens and computer-generated lists. That is the case with both software packages and in-house developments. The new forms of information must be linked with the specific work tasks that are to be supported. At the same time the procedures for performing the tasks need to be redesigned to take full advantage of the potential offered by the new information system. It is, therefore, appropriate to design the system as an integrated extension of business procedures. Since the enterprise model is available in the form of a database, it is a simple matter to add new sources of information and adjust work flows accordingly. In addition, it becomes feasible to develop various alternative designs merely by copying the database and making the desired adjustments.

Another important advantage of a computerized systems model is the possibility of automatically generating financial analyses. Net present value calculations with different time periods and interest rates can be produced with little effort. Cost/benefit analyses for all levels of the organization and various sets of assumptions can be quickly generated and compared. In this way the financial consequences of every alternative can be more thoroughly analyzed, making an optimal systems decision more probable.

8.3 The Use of Reusable Components

If it turns out that an in-house development is the optimal systems decision, the new software should be constructed using a small number of standardized program modules. A large proportion of the modules of any commercial software system can be implemented in the form of reusable components. The advantages of standardized components are well-known in industrial manufacturing: faster production, easier maintenance and low failure rates. For these reasons, the most important module types in every development environment (whether 2GL, 3GL or 4GL) should be standardized. That is the only proven way to achieve productivity gains in programming in the area of 200 per cent to 500 per cent (see Section 1.2.1). Reusable modules developed by experienced programmers are also much more reliable than new modules and have far lower error rates. Reusable, standardized software components make programmer training much easier. Even beginners are able after just a few weeks to develop software systems of a complexity that would otherwise require years of experience to master.

Reusable software components also mean significant advantages for users. User interfaces have a uniform appearance. Programs function in similar and predictable ways. Such homogeneity makes it easier and faster to learn how to use new software systems.

8.4 The Iterative Refinement of the Prototype

Every complex information system, whether an in-house development, a software package or a mixture of the two, is in its first implementation a prototype that must be adjusted to the detailed needs of the organization. The process of adjustment has to be conducted with the aid of the users because no one else has the required detailed knowledge. It is, therefore, advisable to refine the prototype in an iterative fashion with the help of a users' design committee.

During the iterative refinement of a prototype two related problems always surface: controlling the refinement process so that the economic optimum is achieved and limiting the scope of the system to what is financially justifiable. These problems are solved by the analysis of marginal costs and benefits using an enterprise model. In each refinement iteration a particular system release is subjected to a strictly controlled test procedure. At the conclusion of the test suggestions for improvement are discussed in a design committee meeting. The costs for the implementation of the improvement suggestions are compared to the marginal benefits that would be the result of these improvements. If the marginal benefit is not less than the additional costs, then the improvements are implemented, otherwise the existing release is put into production and the refinement phase concluded.

An important factor in the success of prototype refinement is the proper management of the users' design committee. Users' design committees perform three kinds of activities: creative activities, investigative activities and decision-making activities. All three lend themselves to improvement through the application of specific techniques. The creative activities can be supported, for example, by such group design methods as brainstorming or new combinations. Investigative activities can be made easier by such methods as structured information search or user trips. Decision-making and consensus-building are positively influenced by such techniques as classification, objectives trees, check-lists and interaction matrices. It is helpful to brief the members of the users' design committee about the most important group design methods before starting the refinement iterations. That generally makes the committee meetings more productive and positively influences the motivation of the participants.

Controlling the refinement process through the use of marginal cost/benefit analyses and managing the users' design committee with the group design methods offers the best chances for a successful execution of phase 3. The active participation of the users ensures the relevance and acceptance of the system, while the limitation of scope enforced by the marginal cost/benefit analyses guarantees the most economic result.

8.5 Review Questions and Exercises

1. List the most important elements of the three phase method.

2. What are the most important advantages of the use of a database to model the current state of an organization?

3. What are the most important advantages of the use of a database to model a new information system?

4. Why should reusable components be used whenever possible?

5. What is the best way to guarantee a successful execution of phase 3?

Appendix: Review Questions and Exercises with Answers

Chapter 1

1. Name the three most important cost factors in software development.

    (a) Number of source code lines to be delivered.
    (b) Ability of personnel.
    (c) Product complexity.

2. What measures can be taken to reduce the number of deliverable lines of code? What are the advantages and disadvantages of each?

    (a) Use of standard software packages

    Advantages:

    - No programs need to be developed.
    - The programs usually have lower error rate than in-house developments.

    Disadvantages:

    - The software is not tailored to the organization.
    - Adjustments are often impossible, difficult or expensive.

    (b) Use of fourth generation languages

    Advantages:

    - Some types of programs can be programmed more quickly and easily.
    - Well-integrated development environments are frequently available which make testing significantly easier.

    Disadvantages:

    - The languages often exhibit impractical limitations.
    - Hardware utilization is often inefficient, causing response time problems in the production environment.

(c)   Use of reusable software components

Advantages:

- The number of source code lines per programmer per time period can be greatly increased.
- Reusable software components have lower error rates than new modules.

Disadvantages:

- The development of appropriate standards can involve much effort.
- The adherence to standards must be continuously monitored.

(d)   Simplification

Advantages:

- Software systems are easier to create and maintain.
- Simple programs have lower error rates than complex programs.

Disadvantages:

- User requirements are sometimes not completely covered causing acceptance problems.
- Available technical possibilities are not utilized to the fullest extent possible.

3.   Why do users tend to overstate their requirements?

(a)   Because they do not completely understand the functionality of the new system.
(b)   Because they want to enhance the image of their own work group.

4.   Why should end users be involved in the design process?

(a)   Because end users best understand the problems of their work groups.

(b)   Because the participation of users in the design process increases systems' acceptance.

(c)   Because the participation of users in the design process results in greater systems' use.

5.   Discuss the advantages and disadvantages of CASE products.

Advantages:

(a)   A graphic representation of the system can offer a precise and succinct overview of system components.

(b)   Some CASE products force logical consistency among the various systems components.

Disadvantages:

(a)   CASE diagrams are too abstract for many users.

(b)   The interfaces between CASE products are often not sufficiently standardized.

(c)   The quantitative aspects of business problems are not taken into consideration by most CASE products.

6.   Discuss the advantages and disadvantages of prototyping.

Advantages:

(a)   The user does not need to understand abstract design specifications.

(b)   The system designer receives early feedback from user tests and can adjust the system accordingly.

Disadvantages:

(a)   The possibility of future adjustments can result in a superficial attitude toward the analysis of the current system.

(b)   The scope of the improvement process can easily expand beyond what is economically justifiable.

7.   Which programming practices have an important impact on software productivity?

(a)   Application of structured programming techniques.

    (b)   Use of reusable software components.
    (c)   Standardization of all aspects of programs and user interfaces.
    (d)   Centralized maintenance of parameter tables.
    (e)   Use of strong modules.
    (f)   Limitation of number of descendants.
    (g)   Careful management of test environments.

Chapter 2

1. Why does it make sense to develop an enterprise model?

   Because modelling the significant aspects of an organization helps to identify possibilities for improving efficiency.

2. What kinds of information should be included in an enterprise model?

   (a) Strategic data about the long term objectives of the enterprise.
   (b) Operational data about current business procedures.

3. What strategic information should be included in an enterprise model?

   (a) Lists of objectives and subobjectives.
   (b) Lists of problems and possible solutions.

4. What operational information should be included in an enterprise model?

   (a) Job-task-document matrices.
   (b) Lists of tasks with work steps.
   (c) Physical information flows.
   (d) Logical information flows.

5. Name the most important aspects of the structured interview technique in developing an enterprise model.

   (a) Prior determination of the specific information desired.
   (b) Prior determination of the interview procedure.
   (c) Application of different formats for surveying strategic and operational data.

(d) Prior briefing of interviewees.

6. What advantages can be had by storing the enterprise model as a database?

(a) The stored data can be analyzed with the help of computer programs.
(b) The database can be supplemented as needed and updated versions of the reports generated.

7. Discuss the two kinds of benefits provided by information systems and how these can be estimated. Which is usually the more important?

(a) Efficiency gains through reduction in clerical work estimated as work savings per task.
(b) Efficiency gains through improvement of planning and control estimated as an increase in the expected value of a decision situation.

Normally (b) is the more important.

8. Discuss how the critical documents of an organization can be determined.

The critical documents are those that involve tasks with a high potential for improvement and those that are used by many employees.

Chapter 3

1.   List the three categories of files in an applications system.

(a) Applications files.
(b) Table files.
(c) Activity files.

2.   What is the purpose of the activity file?

(a) Exchange of messages.
(b) Sorting and reformatting.

3.   What kinds of information are stored in the table file?

   (a)   Validation information.
   (b)   Process control parameters.
   (c)   Menu information.
   (d)   Help information.
   (e)   Messages (e.g. error messages).

4.   What are the three categories of program in an applications system?

   (a)   Database maintenance programs.
   (b)   List generators.
   (c)   Transformation programs.

5.   List the most important functions of a database maintenance program.

   (a)   Fetch.
   (b)   Scroll forward.
   (c)   Scroll backward.
   (d)   Insert.
   (e)   Alter.
   (f)   Delete.
   (g)   Prepare screen.
   (h)   Help.
   (i)   Table view.
   (j)   End program.

6.   Discuss the most important kinds of processing that transformation
   programs accomplish.

   (a)   Reformatting.
   (b)   Calculation.
   (c)   Sorting.
   (d)   Selection.
   (e)   Summarization.
   (f)   Explosion.
   (g)   Supplementation.

7.   What is a starter program?

A starter program reads requests for batch processes that have been stored in the activity file by interactive programs and initiates the requested processes.

8. What are some of the advantages of using standardized program modules?

    (a) Lower development costs.
    (b) Lower maintenance costs.
    (c) Easier user training.
    (d) Fewer program errors.

Chapter 4

1. What is a primary document?

A primary document is a document that has no source documents. Every logical information flow begins with a primary document.

2. In what kinds of decision processes can information play an essential role?

    (a) Identifying opportunities for the company in the market place.
    (b) Describing the long-range goals and strategies of the company.
    (c) Evaluating goals and strategies.
    (d) Developing marketing systems, manufacturing systems, financial and other systems within the company which are related to the total operational system of the company.
    (e) Developing standards of performance, methods of measurement and methods of control over long-range and operational activities.
    (f) Achieving greater effectiveness (reaching goals) and greater efficiency (decreasing costs).
    (g) Preventing disasters.

3. After analyzing the current system, how are the additional information requirements determined?
    (a) Surveying the managers by traditional means, e.g. with questionnaires or interviews.

(b) Analyzing the decision processes with artificial intelligence
     techniques.
(c) Utilizing standard models and techniques such as those of
     operations research.

4. List the most important steps in the development of a systems
    proposal.

    (a) Determination of total information requirements in terms of lists
         and screens.
    (b) Integration of all users' views.
    (c) Development of data capture strategies.
    (d) Development of data transformation strategies.
    (e) Development of data display strategies.

5. What is the use of a net present value analysis?

    A net present value analysis indicates the value of future cash flows in
    terms of current monetary values.

6. How is the optimal scope of a system determined?

    The information system should be expanded in increments until the
    marginal costs of the next increment equals the marginal benefit
    yielded by that increment.

Chapter 5

1. What are the problems associated with insular system solutions?

    (a) Time delays in the flow of information.
    (b) Costs of interface processing.
    (c) Data inconsistency.

2. What should be the basis for the organization of information and
    why?

Information should be organized by entities because these are less subject to change than the business procedures in which the information is used.

3.   List the most important principles for defining data elements.

(a)   Maximize data element cohesion.
(b)   Minimize data element coupling.
(c)   Standardize data element naming conventions.

4.   What is data independence?

Data independence refers to the separation of the logical and physical aspects of data storage.

5.   Table 5.2 shows a registration form for a seminar. Design a corresponding data model in the third normal form.

For answer see Fig. 5.12 on next page.

Chapter 6

1.   Describe a scientific approach for selecting a software package.

The screens, lists and data structures of each software package under consideration should be entered into a separate enterprise model in exactly the same fashion as the screens, lists and data structures of an in-house development. That means that each information product of the package under investigation must be allocated to the jobs and tasks it is supposed to support in order to see how the organization will function if that package is chosen. The potential savings and anticipated additional effort (= negative savings) should also be determined for each task and stored in the model. On the basis of this information a cost/benefit analysis for each package can be performed. The alternative with the greatest net benefit is the software package of choice.

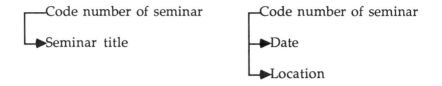

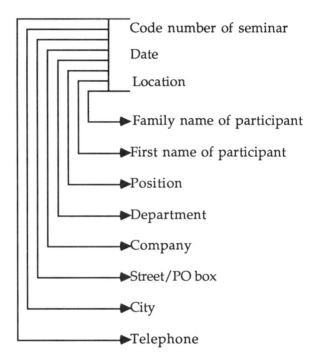

Figure 5.12: Data model for seminar registration

2.   How can standard costing techniques be applied to programming projects?

      The system is constructed from a relatively small number of standardized program models. Past labour statistics are used to work out a standard cost figure for each of these standard components.

3.   How should the sequence of programming be determined?

The sequence of logical information flows should determine the sequence of programming.

4.   What are the basic rules for scheduling programmers?

(a)   The number of programmers should be kept to the absolute minimum consonant with meeting deadlines. When in doubt, use fewer rather than more programmers.
(b)   The division of labour among programmers should be organized such that communication requirements are minimized.

5.   What components should be available in the reusable component library?

(a)   Model programs.
(b)   Screen I/O routines.
(c)   Database access routines.
(d)   Table access routines.
(e)   Date conversion subroutines.
(f)   String manipulation subroutines.
(g)   Statistical and mathematical subroutines.
(h)   Company-specific routines for such things as tax calculations, ageing of accounts, etc.

6.   List the most important steps for software quality control.

(a)   The programmer thoroughly tests his/her programs with realistic test data.
(b)   The library administrator checks the program for adherence to standards.
(c)   The users test the program as part of the iterative refinement process.

7.   What is the main problem in testing and why does it occur?

The main problem in testing is the lack of thoroughness with which the functionality of the software is checked. It results from the following conditions:

(a)   Inadequate amounts of realistic test data.
(b)   Difficulties in the maintenance of the test environment.

(c) Programmers get in each other's way when using the same test environment.

Chapter 7

1. List the most important tasks involved in stepwise refinement.

    (a) Putting the system parts into production and discovering any weaknesses they may have.
    (b) Identifying firm possibilities for improvement that can be implemented with information processing techniques.
    (c) Achieving consensus among different work groups with conflicting interests.
    (d) Limiting the scope of refinement to what is economically justifiable.

2. Why is the use of a design committee an effective way to achieve the necessary cooperation between systems developers and user groups?

    (a) Because of its professional competence.
    (b) Because of its political legitimacy.

3. What are the most important principles for the organization of a design committee?

    (a) Selection of user representative with adequate practical knowledge.
    (b) Preparation of the committee members for their work.
    (c) Delegation to the committee of both responsibility and authority for the definition of the user interface.
    (d) Strict adherence to an exact schedule.

4. List the activities of a refinement iteration.

    (a) Briefing the coordinator.
    (b) Compilation of test data.
    (c) Creation or updating of the user guide.
    (d) Training of the users.
    (e) Testing the prototype.
    (f) Field reports.

(g)   Cost/benefit analysis.
(h)   Design of improvements.
(i)   Implementation of improvements.

5.   What are the three kinds of activities that a design committee performs?

(a)   Investigative activities.
(b)   Creative activities.
(c)   Decision-making activities.

6.   Which design method is appropriate for delegating research tasks? For achieving a consensus about the selection of one of a number of alternatives? For precisely defining system requirements?

(a)   Information search.
(b)   Objectives' trees.
(c)   Performance specification.

7.   Why is a release concept useful?

(a)   To avoid cost overruns.
(b)   To maintain a better overview of the functionality of the system.

8.   How long should the refinement process be continued?

The refinement process should be continued until no further increase in the net marginal utility can be obtained through an improved release.

Chapter 8

1. List the most important elements of the three phase method.

(a)   Enterprise modelling.
(b)   Standardized software components.
(c)   Prototyping.
(d)   Iterative refinement with the help of a design committee.

2. What are the most important advantages of the use of a database to model the current state of an organization?

    (a)   Good overview of strategies, structure, procedures and information.
    (b)   Easy adaptability to organizational change.
    (c)   Automated generation of analyses.

3. What are the most important advantages of the use of a database to model a new information system?

    (a)   Holistic systems planning in terms of real-life organizational procedures.
    (b)   Easy definition of alternatives by copying the database.
    (c)   Automated generation of comparative analyses.

4. Why should reusable components be used whenever possible?

    (a)   Faster programming.
    (b)   Easier maintenance.
    (c)   Lower error rates.

5. What is the best way to guarantee a successful execution of phase 3?

    Controlling the refinement process through marginal analysis of costs and benefits and managing the users' design committee with the group design methods.

Index